Essential
Spiritual Truth

*How to Take Responsibility
for Your Spiritual Destiny*

Robert A. Fusco

Essential Spiritual Truth

How to Take Responsibility
for Your Spiritual Destiny

ISBN 978-1-7353-8390-3
ISBN E-book 978-1-7353-8391-0

With Love from God

Dedication

To all my family that's going to fill the house of God.
May the blessings of heaven be upon you,
and be received by you,
so that you arise to the fullness of all that
God has created you for and called you to do.

"... Truly, I say to you, unless you turn and become like children, you will never enter the kingdom of heaven..."
— Jesus Christ, *Matthew 18:3 (ESV)*

"The simplest soul can touch God and live in the very presence of God and know His power. Man's intellectuality is not an assistant to knowing God. It is rather a detriment. You have to overcome the treacherous knowledge and pride that has been developed in your own soul before you become childlike enough to believe God like a little child does."
— John G. Lake, *The Complete Collection of His Life Teachings*

Contents

In Light of the Times

This book is coincidentally about to be published at a time when the world is in the throes of dealing with the COVID-19 pandemic. This new virus is so easily transmitted that it is wreaking havoc everywhere. Social distancing is being mandated as the primary tool for fighting it, with any wide-scale medical solutions appearing to be months in the future at best. Peak devastation is being neared in certain areas and has yet to be approached in others. The death of loved ones is mounting with heart-breaking speed, while those fighting this virus, especially on the front lines, are being stretched to their limits. The times are filled with unanswered questions, anxiety, frustration and amazement at how extensively this pandemic has so quickly and abruptly changed the world we know. Uncertainty prevails about what the "new normal" will be.

Certainly, there have been many disasters before this one, and no doubt there will be more in the future as well. But perhaps this particular catastrophe is putting an enormous spotlight on mankind's frailty and limited ability to respond to the onslaught of an unforeseen and unknown enemy. Even with advanced technologies, systems and industries, many people are struggling to meet the demands of the day. All these efforts are both necessary and appreciated, but if we persist in assessing things only in the natural realm, we will miss the opportunity to grasp the full picture. Consequently, we will miss the opportunity to deal with life effectively, both on a personal and world-wide level. Short-sightedness will only end in more tragedy, and we will have no one to blame except ourselves. May everyone who reads this book be blessed with eyes to see beyond the immediate and into the eternal.

Introduction

Any effort to understand spiritual things must be heart-driven but with the mind fully engaged. It is the spirit of a person that has the potential to connect with that which is outside the realm of the natural, but that doesn't mean the gears of the brain must be disengaged. Rather, just as with any other exploratory endeavors, greater understanding begins with analysis of what is known already. Then, with perseverance, the knowledge base is expanded which can lead to exciting discoveries. In the spiritual realm, all things revolve around God (even those things in the realm of darkness), so to exclude Him from the effort is to miss the main point.

Fortunately, it seems that most people today still believe that God exists. For them, this book will provide an opportunity to determine if their feet are firmly planted in His reality, or not. The material is taken from the very Word of God, which means that it applies to every individual, whether or not there is any personal connection with Him. And, that application holds true for all who consider themselves members of any formal religion, regardless of whether that association is active or passive, deep or superficial.

For those who would argue that God does not exist, or perhaps are just not sure, this book will provide an opportunity to reevaluate your position. If you are sincerely open to discovering the truth about spiritual matters, I am certain that God will provide the guidance that you need.

Readers with all backgrounds just may find, as did this writer, that some things held dearly as truths are not true at all. And, you just may find the beginning point of the specific road that leads to clarity, where now there is confusion or ignorance or doubt. As you read, hopefully you will grow in your understanding of just who God is, along with what His plans are for today and for the future as well.

For too many years of my life I lived in ignorance of what I now call *essential spiritual truth*. For about the first twenty-one years I acquired information from the lips and writings of others, blindly accepting much of it as irrefutable truth coming from established authorities. I can now see that while much of it was indeed true, some was false, and some critically important things were missing. Most importantly however, even though some of the spiritual knowledge I had gained was accurate, I still lacked understanding of its true significance and of its proper application. To be sure, my character and moral integrity were at least in part positively shaped by what I learned, so there was a real and practical benefit gained. I actively participated in a formal religion, so I had a certain amount of knowledge; still, I lacked the wherewithal to thoroughly apply it to daily living. My acceptance of some false information, along with the absence of some needed information, left me on uncertain ground. I had a definite belief in God, and I had a respectful acceptance of spiritual things, but I was not equipped to move forward with it all in my daily life. Consequently, this religious upbringing became a routine that I would step into, mostly on schedule, briefly participate in, and then return to living my life as usual. There was my natural life, and then there was my spiritual life, but the two were mostly separate entities. Simply speaking, something was missing. I could clearly see the life and death process, but when it came to spiritual things and what, if anything, followed death, well that all was still confusing and mysterious.

Then for about another twenty-one years I simply closed the door on the whole subject. I would say the biggest reason for doing so was a preoccupation with just living life. All the usual things kept me quite busy, such as family, work, additional schooling, property upkeep and entertainment. In the realm of these things I had a degree of focus and application that I could directly relate to, in contrast to otherworldly spiritual concepts. These were the people and things directly in front of me that I could see and touch and which needed attention. It seemed like the spiritual things of "religion" could just be ignored, without any great loss, at least for the time. I still maintained a limited amount of faith in the existence of a God that I could not see or touch, but I made no effort to look for Him. Furthermore, I rationalized that I could decide for myself what was good and bad, right and wrong. I had not come to accept that there really was any specific guideline to follow, so I could just live by my own standard. After all, most everyone else seemed to be doing the same thing, and I figured that my way was as good as any way. Besides, I considered myself to be a relatively good person who tried to live uprightly. So, if God really did exist, surely, He would see that, and it would weigh (hopefully heavily) in my favor; especially with those days and situations in which I was undoubtedly not so upright in His eyes.

What I didn't realize throughout those years is that God is very real and that He has clearly mapped out a way to go for all of mankind, both spiritually and naturally speaking. No surprise, my way at that time was not His way. Thankfully, God saw that I was in desperate need of an intervention and graciously provided me one about 25 years ago. Since then I have been diligently seeking to follow His way rather than my own, and I can assure you that His way is far better indeed.

The overriding intent of my heart with this book is to help you find the beginning point of the road that heads in the right direction. Such a road most definitely exists, just as do the roads which travel in many wrong directions. To be sure, the focus here is to make that beginning point clear, where it has been concealed, confused and unnecessarily clouded in mystery, in the lives of many people. It is just the beginning point, but it is that *essential spiritual truth* which I hope to help you discover.

I so wish that someone had laid these things out for me even when I was a child, but that did not happen. Then years later an opportunity came and went when I was a young adult enjoying a day on the beach. Three young teenagers attempted to talk to me, briefly, about such spiritual things. My religious upbringing enabled me to speak with some knowledge in response to their questions, so they moved on without deeper discussion. I have never forgotten that day because I believe that those children knew some precious truths which I needed to know for myself. With hindsight, I can see that perhaps with a little more openness and a little more perseverance on both of our parts, my entire life could have been radically better. Knowing that with a certainty today, and knowing how priceless these truths are, I want to do my best to present them to you for your consideration. Just like that one-time event on the beach, I realize that this may be the only opportunity I will ever have to make these things plain to you.

Growing up as a child I occasionally heard the comment: "You can lead a horse to water, but you can't make him drink". That is a very old expression but it still has merit in this situation. I will lay out many facts for you, however, whether or not you choose to step out onto that "right" road, or not, is up to you. Having personally spent far too many years on a "wrong" road myself, I can only advise you that from the broad perspective, that time is largely spent wandering aimlessly. No amount of words can convince you that God is real and that He cares about you individually. And, no amount of words can persuade you that what you read here is true. It is not my intention to attempt to do either. However, if you sincerely and with an open heart pursue this process to the end, God Himself will validate the truth of what you read, welcome you with open arms, and equip you to journey on the right road successfully. If I can just help you get started, I will be extremely happy.

Robert A. Fusco

Essential Spiritual Truth

Chapter 1

SEARCHING FOR THE SPIRITUAL

Our lives as human beings have a spiritual as well as a natural component. Probably most people accept that, even though they may have difficulty comprehending it. After all, we readily talk of the human spirit, though we can't quite grasp it like we can the human body because we can't see it or touch it. Never-the-less, life embodies the unity of the two.

Unfortunately, it is far too common for people to keep them separate, like oil and water that don't mix. For example, many will strain to glean some insight from a report of an out-of-body experience, suspecting that something real happened there, just not knowing quite what to do with that glimpse beyond earthly life. Such things raise awareness of a little-known realm, but most people leave it at that and move on. Going back to dealing with the knowable and the doable in the natural realm always seems more practical and necessary.

And there's the more common example of looking to connect with spiritual things by attending a church service. Not always, but too often, it is a formal or routine practice that can leave one with a false sense of security; like somehow a vital spiritual connection was made with the powers beyond, even though there is little or no real understanding of anything that may have transpired.

So again, things in the spiritual arena remain clouded, mysterious, and seemingly unreachable. That being the case, most of us then simply revert to what we know, which are the daily routines of life like work and play. The end result is that natural and spiritual things mostly just seem to flow in separate rivers that rarely, if ever, meet. Yet that is far from the way God designed things to be. His intention has always been that our spiritual and natural lives be tightly woven together, and especially, be united with Him.

Above and Beyond Every Religion

The focal point of this book transcends every formal religion. Doctrines of religious institutions typically consist of a certain amount of truth mixed together with erroneous teachings. That is simply because they are organized and built up by imperfect human beings. Whether false teachings enter in because of good or bad intentions, the result is the same: those who participate in that religion are deceived and their personal lives are, at the very least, diminished by it.

A spiritual life that is centered around an established formal religion can lock one in to its beliefs, guidelines and rituals, which *presumably* will lead one to God and to whatever may be good and waiting for us after death. However, the typical person simply is not equipped to sift through religious teachings to determine what is correct or incorrect. Furthermore, that same typical person is not even motivated to do so. Consequently, the routine practice of any religion can easily end up in mindless participation, with blind trust in the beliefs set forth by those in authority.

While this book contains many references to spiritual teachings, the main objective is to connect the reader directly to the one God who is above any and all religions. Then, out of that relationship can flow the process of learning more of Him and of what His plans, purposes and expectations are. The one who takes this approach becomes increasingly equipped to sift through whatever teaching he is presented with. It is far better to get to know the God of creation first, and let Him be the primary one to lead you into all truth. That is His way of doing things.

Connection with God is Possible

Sadly, there is a horrific, mind-numbing deception which is being promoted throughout the world. Essentially it works to discredit God in any way possible, and it works to persuade all people that, even if they maintain a belief in Him, they are hopelessly disconnected from Him. It reinforces the totally false concept that life on earth takes place in a vacuum, separated from any meaningful communication with Him. It perpetuates the belief that only after the earthly life is ended does one face the possibility of encountering God, with trepidation, for better or for worse.

This is horrifying because it robs people of their freedom to make a choice that has a major and direct bearing on their life. That choice is very simple: get to know God for who He really is, in all His goodness, and live life His way, or not.

Regrettably, there are still a great many people who do not even know that that is a possibility. They simply lack the knowledge that a choice can be made, and so they suffer for it. The option of a choice is subtly removed from the picture by camouflaging its very existence. Of course, there are those who have the knowledge but still refuse to do things God's way; these have already made their choice.

Spiritual + Natural = Completeness

In this fast-moving, information-filled world, it is extremely difficult to capture anyone's attention on any specific point. Without a doubt, more tools are available for communication today than ever before in history. The sheer volume of information, coupled with the speed of transmission, can easily cause any single item to be overwhelmed beyond notice. That being the environment in which we live, the material in this book has been whittled down to the essentials needed to enable you to make that first and priceless direct connection with God Himself.

Beyond what is included here, there is a massive amount of material available in institutions and in the marketplace for more research on any given point. Utilize them if you must, but the reader should keep in mind that this is firstly an exercise of the heart and only secondarily an exercise of the mind. Attempting to understand this material strictly with your mind will not likely yield good results; this is, of course, a spiritual exploration, not a natural one.

Therefore, use your mental capacity to its maximum, but you must also listen with your spirit. Hearing with an open heart and an open mind will produce benefits beyond your greatest expectation. If you are diligent in taking these thoughts further as they apply to your own life, you will have received all the basic ingredients you need to be able to develop these truths into a fullness that will nourish and shape your life forever.

The spiritual things of God, though so widely discredited today, are far more valuable than any other issues of life; though unfortunately it seems that many of us discover the absolute truth of that only after years of wandering. No matter how or when we come to that realization, the joy of living in this world in sync with the One who created it, becomes a beautiful thing. Only then do we begin to make some sense of this world and of our lives.

Look to God, Not Man, for Truth

Without doubt there are many people around who will disagree with some of what you read here. Even so, I am also very confident that there are many people who totally agree with the major issues, if not with it all. No matter what those percentages are, keep in mind that this is all about your own understanding, and that is primarily between you and God. So, throughout the process you should constantly ask God for guidance into His truth so as not to be misled; not by the author or by anyone else. You can do that out loud or silently; either way He will be listening. God will honor your request in this regard and if you are sincere in your efforts, He will faithfully lead you to where you need to go.

Perseverance and acceptance of His truth will bring eternal dividends. Failure to persevere will end with continued ignorance about the spiritual aspect of life. That will be seriously detrimental to you. Besides hurting yourself, you also will have forfeited the opportunity to truly help those you love, or even perfect strangers, because you cannot share what you do not possess.

If you are one who sincerely wants to make the greatest and most positive difference in this world that you can, seek out the One who alone can make it happen. Even the results of the most committed and generous philanthropist will pale in comparison to what may be accomplished when one's efforts are applied in unity with God.

Whatever you do, do it in peace. The contents of this book should stimulate research, discussion and even debate, but all in a spirit of kindness and love. Anyone choosing to make this effort one of hostility is not promoting or searching for Truth, but is attempting to block its discovery. God loves all and does not approve of any behavior that stifles those who are earnestly seeking His way.

About the Bible

Fortunately for all of us human beings, God provided a masterful compilation of documents which is the primary tool we have to seek His way. This is of course, His Holy Bible, which provides us insight into who God is, and what His plans are for now and the coming years as well. It was written by men, but it was divinely inspired by God Himself. Its accuracy and reliability have been proven over many centuries, even though much has been done in an attempt to attack its credibility. That should be expected always, and even more so as time goes by, considering it is the single, most trustworthy source for mankind to live by. It's a manual for getting on board with God and participating with Him in what He wants to do on Earth today.

Numerous references are provided which will direct the reader to the biblical foundation for all key statements made. These references have been carefully selected and intentionally limited, partly for the sake of space but more so for the sake of focus. Use them as is helpful to you to validate the subject of each chapter, and look them up for yourself to study them in the full context in the Bible.

Follow this book to its conclusion and you too will be able to know in your heart that the Bible is a priceless gift from God. We are richly blessed by living in an age when it is made available in a variety of versions, in multiple languages, in print, by audio, on the internet and on smart-device applications also. The information is available at our fingertips and God is more than willing to help us understand it. The Bible is the very Word of God, and to reject it is to reject Him. As you begin to explore what follows, my hope and prayer is that you will treasure His Word and walk in it.

Chapter 2

UNSEEN FRIENDS AND ENEMIES

Even a very broad look into spiritual matters demands some consideration of the subject of angels. Often, they are thought of as simply mythical creatures, more real in one's imagination than in actuality. The truth of the matter though is that at some point God created a large host of angels to serve Him in various ways. They are spiritual beings which are always at work around us and their activities have a direct bearing on people of all nations. Whether it is in the individual, societal or governmental sphere, angels are busy facilitating God's plans throughout both the natural and the spiritual realms.

Powerful Servants

Angels are a class of beings which are quite distinct from human beings. In fact, contrary to some popular thought, human beings don't become angels upon dying. Angels apparently have various degrees of God-given responsibilities, power and authority. For example, they serve as messengers of a word from God to men[1]; they execute the judgments of God[2]; they intervene in the wars of men[3] and certain ones are the closest to God and guard His throne.[4] Although they are spiritual beings that are not normally seen by us, they can become visible[5] and can even manifest as human beings[6].

Rebel Angels

It is hard to understand how these powerful angels, created to serve God and to be in His presence, could ruin such an opportunity; yet that is exactly what happened. A rebellion took place in heaven that was, at least primarily, prompted by pride and led by a high-ranking angel named Lucifer.

Lucifer thought that he was so great that he could exalt himself above God. The result of that rebellion was that Lucifer, now known as Satan or the devil, was cast out of heaven. A third of the angels followed his lead and were cast out as well.[7] Some of these angels have been bound in hell[8], while some still rule today with some power, along with Satan, in spiritual realms over the Earth[9]. Other evil spirits, commonly known as demons, also may derive from the fallen-angel group, though their origin is not perfectly clear. They seem to be more earth-bound, with a driving desire to take up residence in a human being. Once they find a home, they can more fully manifest, which includes the ability to bring on a variety of infirmities in a person.[10]

The fallen angels bound in hell don't seem to have any ability to wreak havoc in the human race for now, but for all the other evil spirits, wherever they exist, their purpose is purely destructive and in opposition to God. That means that they also directly oppose anyone who desires and attempts to live a life that honors God.[11] Even though the fallen angels were ejected from heaven, it appears that their hierarchical structure is still in place, as certain ones have jurisdiction over specific geographical areas of Earth, with the devil ruling over them all.[12] Satan is now called the god or prince of this world and to this day he still exerts significant power within it, though he has only a temporary reprieve from God to do so.[13]

Loyal and Victorious Servants to the End

The remaining two-thirds of the angels that did not rebel against God, continue to serve His purposes in the heavens and on the Earth as directed.[14] Key among the duties of this very large force of good angels, as far as we are concerned, is to assist all those human beings who are endeavoring to fulfill God's purpose for their life and for this world.[15] Furthermore, we can rest assured that the loyal angels of God will be heavily involved in bringing His final plans to conclusion. Even as they continue to honor and worship Him in heaven,[16] they will be instrumental in the release of His end-time catastrophic judgments.[17] Certain ones will announce His way of salvation, together with last-minute warnings for the rebellious to submit to God,[18] and all will continue fighting and overcoming His enemies through to the last battle.[19]

God Permits Evil to Exist

Even with the limited insight we have into this force of angelic beings, we should look at one thing in particular that this whole situation reveals to us about God. It is all too common for mere mortals to look at some of the horrible things going on in the world and to conclude that God cannot possibly exist; or that He is not as powerful as we may like to think; or that if He exists, then He doesn't really know what He's doing.

Here, in the creation and rebellion of angels, we see that even before creation of the world in which we live, God created in such a way that permitted evil to exist. He could certainly have not even made it a possibility, yet He chose to allow it. This alone gives us a peek at the essence of the God who desires to surround Himself with those who love Him and value Him for who He is. He is a God of loving and committed relationship who could, but doesn't, force anyone to follow Him. He is so perfectly and powerfully established in His very existence, that He is quite comfortable allowing evil to exist and to operate in His universe. He does not fear evil and He never has, nor ever will, be overcome by evil.

In fact, though there be many who oppose Him, of both the angelic and the human variety, God is expert at using their best efforts to serve His purposes. He has a long-term perspective and strategy which excludes the possibility that things will always be this way. However, for now, even the most aggressive and determined plans of His enemies only serve to facilitate the end He has at heart. All God's enemies are His own creations turned rebels, but while this spiritual variety still has some God-given power, ultimate authority rests solely with God Himself. He alone is sovereign and in complete control.

Chapter 2 References:

1 * * *
Judges 13:3 (ESV)
3 And the angel of the LORD appeared to the woman and said to her, "Behold, you are barren and have not borne children, but you shall conceive and bear a son.

Luke 1:26-28
26 Now in the sixth month, the angel Gabriel was sent from God to a city of Galilee named Nazareth, 27 to a virgin pledged to be married to a man whose name was Joseph, of David's house. The

virgin's name was Mary. 28 Having come in, the angel said to her, "Rejoice, you highly favored one! The Lord is with you. Blessed are you among women!"

2 * * *

Genesis 19:12-13 (ESV)
12 Then the men said to Lot, "Have you anyone else here? Sons-in-law, sons, daughters, or anyone you have in the city, bring them out of the place. 13 For we are about to destroy this place, because the outcry against its people has become great before the LORD, and the LORD has sent us to destroy it."

2 Samuel 24:15-16 (ESV)
15 So the LORD sent a pestilence on Israel from the morning until the appointed time. And there died of the people from Dan to Beersheba 70,000 men. 16 And when the angel stretched out his hand toward Jerusalem to destroy it, the LORD relented from the calamity and said to the angel who was working destruction among the people, "It is enough; now stay your hand." And the angel of the LORD was by the threshing floor of Araunah the Jebusite.

3 * * *

2 Kings 19:35 (ESV)
35 And that night the angel of the LORD went out and struck down 185,000 in the camp of the Assyrians. And when people arose early in the morning, behold, these were all dead bodies.

2 Chronicles 32:20-21 (ESV)
20 Then Hezekiah the king and Isaiah the prophet, the son of Amoz, prayed because of this and cried to heaven. 21 And the LORD sent an angel, who cut off all the mighty warriors and commanders and officers in the camp of the king of Assyria. So he returned with shame of face to his own land. And when he came into the house of his god, some of his own sons struck him down there with the sword.

4 * * *

Isaiah 6:1-2

In the year that king Uzziah died, I saw the Lord sitting on a throne, high and lifted up; and his train filled the temple. [2] Above him stood the seraphim. Each one had six wings. With two he covered his face. With two he covered his feet. With two he flew.

[5] * * *

Luke 1:11-12

[11] An angel of the Lord appeared to him, standing on the right side of the altar of incense. [12] Zacharias was troubled when he saw him, and fear fell upon him.

Luke 2:8-9

[8] There were shepherds in the same country staying in the field, and keeping watch by night over their flock. [9] Behold, an angel of the Lord stood by them, and the glory of the Lord shone around them, and they were terrified.

[6] * * *

Genesis 18:1-2 (ESV)

[1] And the LORD appeared to him by the oaks of Mamre, as he sat at the door of his tent in the heat of the day. [2] He lifted up his eyes and looked, and behold, three men were standing in front of him. When he saw them, he ran from the tent door to meet them and bowed himself to the earth

Genesis 18:21-22 (ESV)

[21] I will go down to see whether they have done altogether according to the outcry that has come to me. And if not, I will know." [22] So the men turned from there and went toward Sodom, but Abraham still stood before the LORD.

Genesis 19:1-2

The two angels came to Sodom at evening. Lot sat in the gate of Sodom. Lot saw them, and rose up to meet them. He bowed himself with his face to the earth, [2] and he said, "See now, my lords, please come into your servant's house, stay all night, wash your feet, and you can rise up early, and go on your way." They said, "No, but we will stay in the street all night."

7 * * *

Isaiah 14:12-15

12 How you have fallen from heaven, shining one, son of the dawn! How you are cut down to the ground, who laid the nations low! 13 You said in your heart, "I will ascend into heaven! I will exalt my throne above the stars of God! I will sit on the mountain of assembly, in the far north! 14 I will ascend above the heights of the clouds! I will make myself like the Most High!" 15 Yet you shall be brought down to Sheol, (Sheol is the place of the dead) to the depths of the pit.

Revelation 12:3-4

3 Another sign was seen in heaven. Behold, a great red dragon, having seven heads and ten horns, and on his heads seven crowns. 4 His tail drew one third of the stars of the sky, and threw them to the earth. The dragon stood before the woman who was about to give birth, so that when she gave birth he might devour her child.

8 * * *

Jude 1:6

6 Angels who didn't keep their first domain, but deserted their own dwelling place, he has kept in everlasting bonds under darkness for the judgment of the great day.

2 Peter 2:4

4 For if God didn't spare angels when they sinned, but cast them down to Tartarus, (Tartarus is another name for Hell) and committed them to pits of darkness to be reserved for judgment;

9 * * *

Ephesians 1:19-21

19 and what is the exceeding greatness of his power toward us who believe, according to that working of the strength of his might 20 which he worked in Christ, when he raised him from the dead and made him to sit at his right hand in the heavenly places, 21 far above all rule, authority, power, dominion, and every name that is named, not only in this age, but also in that which is to come.

Ephesians 6:12

12 For our wrestling is not against flesh and blood, but against the principalities, against the powers, against the world's rulers of the darkness of this age, and against the spiritual forces of wickedness in the heavenly places.

10 * * *

Matthew 9:32-33

32 As they went out, behold, a mute man who was demon possessed was brought to him. 33 When the demon was cast out, the mute man spoke. The multitudes marveled, saying, "Nothing like this has ever been seen in Israel!"

Mark 16:9

9 Now when he had risen early on the first day of the week, he appeared first to Mary Magdalene, from whom he had cast out seven demons.

Luke 9:42

42 While he was still coming, the demon threw him down and convulsed him violently. But Jesus rebuked the unclean spirit, healed the boy, and gave him back to his father.

1 Timothy 4:1

But the Spirit says expressly that in later times some will fall away from the faith, paying attention to seducing spirits and doctrines of demons,

11 * * *

Mark 7:26-30

26 Now the woman was a Greek, a Syrophoenician by race. She begged him that he would cast the demon out of her daughter. 27 But Jesus said to her, "Let the children be filled first, for it is not appropriate to take the children's bread and throw it to the dogs." 28 But she answered him, "Yes, Lord. Yet even the dogs under the table eat the children's crumbs." 29 He said to her, "For this saying, go your way. The demon has gone out of your daughter." 30 She went away to her house, and found the child having been laid on the bed, with the demon gone out.

1 Corinthians 10:20-21
20 But I say that the things which the Gentiles sacrifice, they sacrifice to demons, and not to God, and I don't desire that you would have fellowship with demons. 21 You can't both drink the cup of the Lord and the cup of demons. You can't both partake of the table of the Lord and of the table of demons.

12 * * *

Daniel 10:12-13
12 Then he said to me, "Don't be afraid, Daniel; for from the first day that you set your heart to understand, and to humble yourself before your God, your words were heard. I have come for your words' sake. 13 But the prince of the kingdom of Persia withstood me twenty-one days; but, behold, Michael, one of the chief princes, came to help me because I remained there with the kings of Persia.

Daniel 10:20
20 Then he said, "Do you know why I have come to you? Now I will return to fight with the prince of Persia. When I go out, behold, the prince of Greece will come.

Matthew 4:8-9
8 Again, the devil took him to an exceedingly high mountain, and showed him all the kingdoms of the world and their glory. 9 He said to him, "I will give you all of these things, if you will fall down and worship me."

13 * * * *

2 Corinthians 4:3-4
3 Even if our Good News is veiled, it is veiled in those who are dying, 4 in whom the god of this world has blinded the minds of the unbelieving, that the light of the Good News of the glory of Christ, who is the image of God, should not dawn on them.

1 John 5:19
19 We know that we are of God, and the whole world lies in the power of the evil one.

14 * * *

Matthew 26:53
53 Or do you think that I couldn't ask my Father, and he would even now send me more than twelve legions of angels?

Mark 8:38
38 For whoever will be ashamed of me and of my words in this adulterous and sinful generation, the Son of Man also will be ashamed of him, when he comes in his Father's glory, with the holy angels."

Acts 12:6-7
6 The same night when Herod was about to bring him out, Peter was sleeping between two soldiers, bound with two chains. Guards in front of the door kept the prison. 7 And behold, an angel of the Lord stood by him, and a light shone in the cell. He struck Peter on the side, and woke him up, saying, "Stand up quickly!" His chains fell off his hands.

15 * * *

Psalm 34:7 (ESV)
7 The angel of the LORD encamps around those who fear him, and delivers them.

Hebrews 1:13-14
But which of the angels has he told at any time, "Sit at my right hand, until I make your enemies the footstool of your feet?" 14 Aren't they all serving spirits, sent out to do service for the sake of those who will inherit salvation?

16 * * *

Revelation 5:11
11 I saw, and I heard something like a voice of many angels around the throne, the living creatures, and the elders. The number of them was ten thousands of ten thousands, and thousands of thousands;

Revelation 7:11

11 All the angels were standing around the throne, the elders, and the four living creatures; and they fell on their faces before his throne, and worshiped God,

17 * * *

Revelation 9:1-3

The fifth angel sounded, and I saw a star from the sky which had fallen to the earth. The key to the pit of the abyss was given to him. 2 He opened the pit of the abyss, and smoke went up out of the pit, like the smoke from a burning furnace. The sun and the air were darkened because of the smoke from the pit. 3 Then out of the smoke came locusts on the earth, and power was given to them, as the scorpions of the earth have power.

Revelation 16:4-6

4 The third poured out his bowl into the rivers and springs of water, and they became blood. 5 I heard the angel of the waters saying, "You are righteous, who are and who were, O Holy One, because you have judged these things. 6 For they poured out the blood of saints and prophets, and you have given them blood to drink. They deserve this."

18 * * *

Revelation 14:6-7

6 I saw an angel flying in mid heaven, having an eternal Good News to proclaim to those who dwell on the earth, and to every nation, tribe, language, and people. 7 He said with a loud voice, "Fear the Lord, and give him glory; for the hour of his judgment has come. Worship him who made the heaven, the earth, the sea, and the springs of waters!"

19 * * *

Revelation 12:7-9

7 There was war in the sky. Michael and his angels made war on the dragon. The dragon and his angels made war. 8 They didn't prevail. No place was found for them any more in heaven. 9 The great dragon was thrown down, the old serpent, he who is called the devil and Satan, the deceiver of the whole world. He was

thrown down to the earth, and his angels were thrown down with him.

Revelation 19:11-14

[11] I saw the heaven opened, and behold, a white horse, and he who sat on it is called Faithful and True. In righteousness he judges and makes war. [12] His eyes are a flame of fire, and on his head are many crowns. He has names written and a name written which no one knows but he himself. [13] He is clothed in a garment sprinkled with blood. His name is called "The Word of God." [14] The armies which are in heaven followed him on white horses, clothed in white, pure, fine linen.

Chapter 3

MANDATORY SEPARATION

God created all that we know and see and appreciate on Earth and in the heavens and in the seas.[1] Then He created the first man and woman, Adam and Eve, and put them in a garden He planted in Eden, charging them to be fruitful and multiply.[2] His creation was perfect and He was very pleased with it, including mankind at that point.[3] Man was given the distinct position and privilege of overseeing the creation as God's representatives. Originally man had direct and open communication with God, in a perfect environment, all made for eternity. God created human beings in His own image, so He gave man a free will, not wanting a world full of robotic people who simply did whatever He directed.[4]

Rebellious Man

That's the way it was intended to be for all mankind; unfortunately, things turned out much differently. God gave Adam a command not to eat the fruit of just one specific tree in the garden, otherwise he would die.[5] However, that disastrous moment came when Adam and Eve chose to ignore His command, exercising their free will to their own loss and to the loss of every one of their descendants (like you and me). Satan, manifesting himself through a serpent, deceived the woman, and the man followed her lead, disobeying God's command. Satan convinced Eve that they would not die and that they could be wise like God.[6] Adam and Eve chose to believe the lie of Satan rather than trust in God and the result was that their close and intimate relationship with God was broken.

Since then all men have had to labor for their provision and all women have had to suffer increased pain in childbearing.[7] This act of disobedience to God brought an abrupt end to that perfect environment.[8] The first parents of mankind were cast out of the Garden of Eden. They were forbidden to enter it again, being excluded from God's presence just as the fallen angels had to be excluded.[9] God's perfect creation became spiritually polluted so that life, once created for eternity, would now have to face death.[10] The failure of Adam and Eve to be obedient to God brought disastrous corruption to humanity and even to the rest of creation.[11] The extent of the damage done can be seen immediately in the life of their first son, who committed the first murder in the history of man, killing his own brother.[12]

Sin Requires Separation from God

Therefore, let's note well these two things: First, today all humanity lives in a natural world system that is heavily influenced from a spiritual dimension by an enemy of God and those who serve him.[13] Second, every individual, from conception and birth into this world, is fallen from God's original perfect design and is thereby restricted from being in God's presence[14] (except for young children who die prematurely). Because of these things all are prone to rebel against God and so all are also enemies of God, unless we seek His favor to make things different.[15]

Either of those things by themselves is a major handicap, but the combination of the two presents what seems to be an insurmountable problem. We live in a world pressured by unseen evil spiritual beings intent on keeping us from God, and, our fallen nature so debilitates us that we are greatly hindered in exerting any real authority, on our own, to correct the situation. Because of the corruption brought into the world by the bad choice of the first human beings, all of mankind, along with all of nature, was plunged into a mode of life ending with death that continues to this day.[16]

Although God created man to live forever, obviously the ever-present reality of death surrounds us. For a while following the Fall, man lived for hundreds of years and now his life span is dramatically shortened, most often to less than one hundred years.[17] Physical death continues to take its toll throughout the world, yet we will see later that eternal life, that is life forever with God beyond physical death, remains as an option for anyone who seeks it.[18]

God's ways are far above man's ways; His power and goodness and wisdom are amazing.[19] Angels turned away from Him, yet He still utilizes their evil deeds to facilitate His ultimate purposes. Man turned away from the Creator also, yet God still has made a way for all of us to draw near to Him and to work with Him in this very day and for all eternity.

Chapter 3 References:

[1] * * *
Genesis 1:1-5
In the beginning, God created the heavens and the earth. [2] The earth was formless and empty. Darkness was on the surface of the

deep and God's Spirit was hovering over the surface of the waters.³ God said, "Let there be light," and there was light. ⁴ God saw the light, and saw that it was good. God divided the light from the darkness. ⁵ God called the light "day", and the darkness he called "night". There was evening and there was morning, the first day.

Isaiah 48:12-13
"Listen to me, O Jacob, and Israel my called: I am he. I am the first. I am also the last. ¹³ Yes, my hand has laid the foundation of the earth, and my right hand has spread out the heavens. When I call to them, they stand up together.

2 * * *

Genesis 1:26-28
²⁶ God said, "Let's make man in our image, after our likeness. Let them have dominion over the fish of the sea, and over the birds of the sky, and over the livestock, and over all the earth, and over every creeping thing that creeps on the earth." ²⁷ God created man in his own image. In God's image he created him; male and female he created them. ²⁸ God blessed them. God said to them, "Be fruitful, multiply, fill the earth, and subdue it. Have dominion over the fish of the sea, over the birds of the sky, and over every living thing that moves on the earth."

Genesis 2:7-8 (ESV)
⁷ then the LORD God formed the man of dust from the ground and breathed into his nostrils the breath of life, and the man became a living creature. ⁸ And the LORD God planted a garden in Eden, in the east, and there he put the man whom he had formed.

Genesis 2:21-23 (ESV)
²¹ So the LORD God caused a deep sleep to fall upon the man, and while he slept took one of his ribs and closed up its place with flesh. ²² And the rib that the LORD God had taken from the man he made into a woman and brought her to the man. ²³ Then the man said, "This at last is bone of my bones and flesh of my flesh; she shall be called Woman, because she was taken out of Man."

---

3 * * *

Genesis 1:31
31 God saw everything that he had made, and, behold, it was very good. There was evening and there was morning, a sixth day.

4 * * *

Genesis 1:26
26 God said, "Let's make man in our image, after our likeness. Let them have dominion over the fish of the sea, and over the birds of the sky, and over the livestock, and over all the earth, and over every creeping thing that creeps on the earth."

Genesis 2:15 (ESV)
15 The LORD God took the man and put him in the garden of Eden to work it and keep it.

Genesis 2:19 (ESV)
19 Now out of the ground the LORD God had formed every beast of the field and every bird of the heavens and brought them to the man to see what he would call them. And whatever the man called every living creature, that was its name.

5 * * *

Genesis 2:16-17 (ESV)
16 And the LORD God commanded the man, saying, "You may surely eat of every tree of the garden, 17 but of the tree of the knowledge of good and evil you shall not eat, for in the day that you eat of it you shall surely die."

6 * * *

Genesis 3:1-6 (ESV)
1 Now the serpent was more crafty than any other beast of the field that the LORD God had made. He said to the woman, "Did God actually say, 'You shall not eat of any tree in the garden'?" 2 And the woman said to the serpent, "We may eat of the fruit of the trees in the garden, 3 but God said, 'You shall not eat of the fruit of the tree that is in the midst of the garden, neither shall you touch it, lest you die.'" 4 But the serpent said to the woman, "You will not surely die. 5 For God knows that when you eat of it your eyes will

be opened, and you will be like God, knowing good and evil." 6 So when the woman saw that the tree was good for food, and that it was a delight to the eyes, and that the tree was to be desired to make one wise, she took of its fruit and ate, and she also gave some to her husband who was with her, and he ate.

7 * * *
Genesis 3:16-19
16 To the woman he said, "I will greatly multiply your pain in childbirth. You will bear children in pain. Your desire will be for your husband, and he will rule over you." 17 To Adam he said, "Because you have listened to your wife's voice, and have eaten from the tree, about which I commanded you, saying, 'You shall not eat of it,' the ground is cursed for your sake. You will eat from it with much labor all the days of your life. 18 It will yield thorns and thistles to you; and you will eat the herb of the field. 19 You will eat bread by the sweat of your face until you return to the ground, for you were taken out of it. For you are dust, and you shall return to dust."

8 * * *
Genesis 2:25
25 The man and his wife were both naked, and they were not ashamed.

Genesis 3:7-8 (ESV)
7 Then the eyes of both were opened, and they knew that they were naked. And they sewed fig leaves together and made themselves loincloths. 8 And they heard the sound of the LORD God walking in the garden in the cool of the day, and the man and his wife hid themselves from the presence of the LORD God among the trees of the garden.

9 * * *
Genesis 3:22-24 (ESV)
22 Then the LORD God said, "Behold, the man has become like one of us in knowing good and evil. Now, lest he reach out his hand and take also of the tree of life and eat, and live forever—" 23 therefore the LORD God sent him out from the garden of Eden to

work the ground from which he was taken. 24 He drove out the man, and at the east of the garden of Eden he placed the cherubim and a flaming sword that turned every way to guard the way to the tree of life.

10 * * *

Genesis 3:19
19 You will eat bread by the sweat of your face until you return to the ground, for you were taken out of it. For you are dust, and you shall return to dust."

Romans 5:12
12 Therefore as sin entered into the world through one man, and death through sin; so death passed to all men, because all sinned.

Romans 6:23
23 For the wages of sin is death, but the free gift of God is eternal life in Christ Jesus our Lord.

11 * * *

Genesis 3:14 (ESV)
14 The LORD God said to the serpent, "Because you have done this, cursed are you above all livestock and above all beasts of the field; on your belly you shall go, and dust you shall eat all the days of your life.

Genesis 3:17-18
17 To Adam he said, "Because you have listened to your wife's voice, and have eaten from the tree, about which I commanded you, saying, 'You shall not eat of it,' the ground is cursed for your sake. You will eat from it with much labor all the days of your life. 18 It will yield thorns and thistles to you; and you will eat the herb of the field.

Romans 8:20-21
20 For the creation was subjected to vanity, not of its own will, but because of him who subjected it, in hope 21 that the creation itself also will be delivered from the bondage of decay into the liberty of the glory of the children of God.

12 * * *

Genesis 4:6-8 (ESV)
6 The LORD said to Cain, "Why are you angry, and why has your face fallen? 7 If you do well, will you not be accepted? And if you do not do well, sin is crouching at the door. Its desire is for you, but you must rule over it." 8 Cain spoke to Abel his brother. And when they were in the field, Cain rose up against his brother Abel and killed him.

13 * * *

2 Corinthians 4:3-4
3 Even if our Good News is veiled, it is veiled in those who are dying, 4 in whom the god of this world has blinded the minds of the unbelieving, that the light of the Good News of the glory of Christ, who is the image of God, should not dawn on them.

1 Peter 5:8
8 Be sober and self-controlled. Be watchful. Your adversary, the devil, walks around like a roaring lion, seeking whom he may devour.

14 * * *

Psalm 51:5
5 Behold, I was born in iniquity. My mother conceived me in sin.

Isaiah 59:1-2 (ESV)
1 Behold, the LORD's hand is not shortened, that it cannot save, or his ear dull, that it cannot hear; 2 but your iniquities have made a separation between you and your God, and your sins have hidden his face from you so that he does not hear.

Proverbs 22:15
15 Folly is bound up in the heart of a child: the rod of discipline drives it far from him.

15 * * *
Ephesians 2:1-3

 You were made alive when you were dead in transgressions and sins, ²in which you once walked according to the course of this world, according to the prince of the power of the air, the spirit who now works in the children of disobedience. ³We also all once lived among them in the lusts of our flesh, doing the desires of the flesh and of the mind, and were by nature children of wrath, even as the rest.

Matthew 15:18-19
¹⁸But the things which proceed out of the mouth come out of the heart, and they defile the man. ¹⁹For out of the heart come evil thoughts, murders, adulteries, sexual sins, thefts, false testimony, and blasphemies.

16 * * *

Ezekiel 18:4
⁴Behold, all souls are mine; as the soul of the father, so also the soul of the son is mine. The soul who sins, he shall die.

James 1:12-15
¹²Blessed is a person who endures temptation, for when he has been approved, he will receive the crown of life, which the Lord promised to those who love him. ¹³Let no man say when he is tempted, "I am tempted by God," for God can't be tempted by evil, and he himself tempts no one. ¹⁴But each one is tempted when he is drawn away by his own lust and enticed. ¹⁵Then the lust, when it has conceived, bears sin. The sin, when it is full grown, produces death.

17 * * *

Genesis 5:3-5
³Adam lived one hundred thirty years, and became the father of a son in his own likeness, after his image, and named him Seth. ⁴The days of Adam after he became the father of Seth were eight hundred years, and he became the father of other sons and daughters. ⁵All the days that Adam lived were nine hundred thirty years, then he died.

Psalm 90:10

---

[10] The days of our years are seventy, or even by reason of strength eighty years; yet their pride is but labor and sorrow, for it passes quickly, and we fly away.

[18] * * *

Isaiah 25:8-9 (ESV)
[8] He will swallow up death forever; and the Lord GOD will wipe away tears from all faces, and the reproach of his people he will take away from all the earth, for the LORD has spoken. [9] It will be said on that day, "Behold, this is our God; we have waited for him, that he might save us. This is the LORD; we have waited for him; let us be glad and rejoice in his salvation."

John 14:1-3
"Don't let your heart be troubled. Believe in God. Believe also in me. [2] In my Father's house are many homes. If it weren't so, I would have told you. I am going to prepare a place for you. [3] If I go and prepare a place for you, I will come again, and will receive you to myself; that where I am, you may be there also.

[19] * * *

Isaiah 55:8-9 (ESV)
[8] For my thoughts are not your thoughts, neither are your ways my ways, declares the LORD. [9] For as the heavens are higher than the earth, so are my ways higher than your ways and my thoughts than your thoughts.

Psalm 103:8-14 (ESV)
[8] The LORD is merciful and gracious, slow to anger and abounding in steadfast love. [9] He will not always chide, nor will he keep his anger forever. [10] He does not deal with us according to our sins, nor repay us according to our iniquities. [11] For as high as the heavens are above the earth, so great is his steadfast love toward those who fear him; [12] as far as the east is from the west, so far does he remove our transgressions from us. [13] As a father shows compassion to his children, so the LORD shows compassion to those who fear him. [14] For he knows our frame; he remembers that we are dust.

Chapter 4

PERFECT JUSTICE PREVAILS

On every conceivable point of that which is good, God shines with excellence beyond man's understanding. Even though man is made in God's image, there is no comparison between man in his fallen condition and the Creator. God does everything with perfection. He loves perfectly[1], as well as unconditionally, which means that He loves even those who hate Him[2]. He knows the heart of the matter and of the person and cannot be deceived[3]. He is all powerful[4], all knowing[5], omnipresent[6], totally just[7] and perfectly holy[8]. He does not strive to cultivate and manifest such things like a man "tries to be good"; He simply IS all of these things and so much more in His very nature. These few words alone hardly do Him any kind of justice, yet it's worth taking a moment to contemplate Someone so perfect on even these few points.

Sin Is Not Relative

And on that point of His holiness we need now to dig deeper into this matter of sin. It is not a popular word or subject to be sure; and increasingly, it seems to be becoming a word considered archaic, of variable meaning, and worse, of no meaning or value at all. However just as the nature of God is unchanging, so too is the nature of sin.[9] As mere men and women we are adept at measuring our moral and ethical behavior relative to our personal standard of right and wrong, which typically has a lot of fudge factor in it. And this standard is in varying measure derived from our judgment of the behavior of others. Consequently, we often and easily conclude that our speech and our behaviors are not as bad as the next person. So, we also conclude that in God's eyes, we must be "okay", since He must surely count this "relative goodness" to our credit.[10]

But the reality is that if we stack ourselves against the perfect, excellent, superlative God that I previously and ever so briefly described, we would quickly see that our lives are like a black splotch of paint tossed onto an exquisite painting. That horrid splotch simply has no place there and would make anyone recoil at the sight, especially the artist himself.[11] Now that is the truth of how we need to view our sinful lives relative to God's standard of perfection.

Sin Pervades All Humanity

Generally speaking, sin is anything that is offensive to God and rebels against His righteous standard, whether it is in thought or deed. And the things that we don't do, that we should do, are not any less offensive to Him. God's very life and nature are what set the mark in all things; sin manifests every time we miss that mark.[12] Weighing ourselves against the lives of other sinful men is total foolishness and a self-deception. Certainly, some sin is worse than others, but the presence of any sin at all, however seemingly trivial, is enough to demand separation from a perfectly holy God[13].

So even the things that many people would be inclined to chalk off as insignificant, such as a lie, or a lustful thought or the theft of an inexpensive item, are offensive to God and therefore are sins[14]. Think back to Adam and Eve and their eating the fruit of a tree. That simple act sounds insignificant to us today, yet it was a huge mistake that affected the entire human race. So however unpopular the word may be, sin is a very real and significant part of everyone's life. We come into this world with the corrupted nature of our first parents and so we all do things which fall short of God's perfection.[15]

God Judges Perfectly

Another foolish self-deception, and one that many put their hope in, is that since God is good and loving He certainly could not, and would not, reject anyone. This thought process, fabricated by the mind of man, simply does not line up with the character of God as revealed in His Holy Scriptures. As with everything else He does perfectly, God judges perfectly also. Therefore, all sin must be punished and sin results in death[16]. In the natural our bodies physically die after a relatively short time, and in the spiritual, death means eternal separation from God.

God simply cannot and will not abide with anything less than His own perfect nature.[17] This fact leaves mankind in an impossible situation, except for the reality that with God all things are possible[18]. So, we will look at God's solution to man's problem shortly, but first it's valuable to look back at a couple of more slices of history. These brief snapshots say much about man's efforts to do things on his own, driven by rebellion, and God's response.

_____

Chapter 4 References:

_____

45

1 * * *

Psalm 136:5

5 to him who by understanding made the heavens; for his loving kindness endures forever:

1 John 4:7-10

7 Beloved, let's love one another, for love is of God; and everyone who loves has been born of God, and knows God. 8 He who doesn't love doesn't know God, for God is love. 9 By this God's love was revealed in us, that God has sent his one and only Son into the world that we might live through him. 10 In this is love, not that we loved God, but that he loved us, and sent his Son as the atoning sacrifice for our sins.

2 * * *

Luke 23:33-34

33 When they came to the place that is called "The Skull", they crucified him there with the criminals, one on the right and the other on the left. 34 Jesus said, "Father, forgive them, for they don't know what they are doing." Dividing his garments among them, they cast lots.

John 3:16-17

16 For God so loved the world, that he gave his one and only Son, that whoever believes in him should not perish, but have eternal life. 17 For God didn't send his Son into the world to judge the world, but that the world should be saved through him.

3 * * *

1 Kings 8:39

39 then hear in heaven, your dwelling place, and forgive, and act, and give to every man according to all his ways, whose heart you know (for you, even you only, know the hearts of all the children of men);

1 John 3:20

20 because if our heart condemns us, God is greater than our heart, and knows all things.

Proverbs 5:21 (ESV)
[21] For a man's ways are before the eyes of the LORD, and he ponders all his paths.

4 * * *

Job 42:2
[2] "I know that you can do all things, and that no purpose of yours can be restrained.

Philippians 3:21
[21] who will change the body of our humiliation to be conformed to the body of his glory, according to the working by which he is able even to subject all things to himself.

Revelation 1:8
[8] "I am the Alpha and the Omega, " says the Lord God, "who is and who was and who is to come, the Almighty."

5 * * *

Psalm 94:9-11 (ESV)
[9] He who planted the ear, does he not hear? He who formed the eye, does he not see? [10] He who disciplines the nations, does he not rebuke? He who teaches man knowledge— [11] the LORD—knows the thoughts of man, that they are but a breath.

Proverbs 24:12
[12] If you say, "Behold, we didn't know this," doesn't he who weighs the hearts consider it? He who keeps your soul, doesn't he know it? Shall he not render to every man according to his work?

Matthew 6:8
[8] Therefore don't be like them, for your Father knows what things you need before you ask him.

6 * * *

Matthew 18:20
[20] For where two or three are gathered together in my name, there I am in the middle of them."

Matthew 28:20

20 teaching them to observe all things that I commanded you. Behold, I am with you always, even to the end of the age." Amen.

Psalm 139:7-12

7 Where could I go from your Spirit? Or where could I flee from your presence? 8 If I ascend up into heaven, you are there. If I make my bed in Sheol, (Sheol is the place of the dead) behold, you are there! 9 If I take the wings of the dawn, and settle in the uttermost parts of the sea, 10 even there your hand will lead me, and your right hand will hold me. 11 If I say, "Surely the darkness will overwhelm me. The light around me will be night," 12 even the darkness doesn't hide from you, but the night shines as the day. The darkness is like light to you.

7 * * *

Deuteronomy 32:4

4 The Rock: his work is perfect, for all his ways are just. A God of faithfulness who does no wrong, just and right is he.

Psalm 9:7-9 (ESV)

7 But the LORD sits enthroned forever; he has established his throne for justice, 8 and he judges the world with righteousness; he judges the peoples with uprightness. 9 The LORD is a stronghold for the oppressed, a stronghold in times of trouble.

Romans 1:18

18 For the wrath of God is revealed from heaven against all ungodliness and unrighteousness of men who suppress the truth in unrighteousness,

John 5:30

30 I can of myself do nothing. As I hear, I judge, and my judgment is righteous; because I don't seek my own will, but the will of my Father who sent me.

8 * * *

Psalm 99:1-3 (ESV)

---

[1] The LORD reigns; let the peoples tremble! He sits enthroned upon the cherubim; let the earth quake! [2] The LORD is great in Zion; he is exalted over all the peoples. [3] Let them praise your great and awesome name! Holy is he!

Hebrews 7:26
[26] For such a high priest was fitting for us: holy, guiltless, undefiled, separated from sinners, and made higher than the heavens;

1 Peter 1:14-16
[14] as children of obedience, not conforming yourselves according to your former lusts as in your ignorance, [15] but just as he who called you is holy, you yourselves also be holy in all of your behavior; [16] because it is written, "You shall be holy; for I am holy."

9 * * *

Ecclesiastes 9:3
[3] This is an evil in all that is done under the sun, that there is one event to all: yes also, the heart of the sons of men is full of evil, and madness is in their heart while they live, and after that they go to the dead.

Jeremiah 17:9
[9] The heart is deceitful above all things and it is exceedingly corrupt. Who can know it?

Romans 8:6-7
[6] For the mind of the flesh is death, but the mind of the Spirit is life and peace; [7] because the mind of the flesh is hostile toward God; for it is not subject to God's law, neither indeed can it be.

1 John 3:4
[4] Everyone who sins also commits lawlessness. Sin is lawlessness.

10 * * *

Luke 18:9-14
[9] He also spoke this parable to certain people who were convinced of their own righteousness, and who despised all others. [10] "Two

men went up into the temple to pray; one was a Pharisee, and the other was a tax collector. [11] The Pharisee stood and prayed to himself like this: 'God, I thank you that I am not like the rest of men, extortionists, unrighteous, adulterers, or even like this tax collector. [12] I fast twice a week. I give tithes of all that I get.' [13] But the tax collector, standing far away, wouldn't even lift up his eyes to heaven, but beat his breast, saying, 'God, be merciful to me, a sinner!' [14] I tell you, this man went down to his house justified rather than the other; for everyone who exalts himself will be humbled, but he who humbles himself will be exalted."

[11] * * *

Psalm 14:1-3 (ESV)
[1] The fool says in his heart, "There is no God." They are corrupt, they do abominable deeds, there is none who does good. [2] The LORD looks down from heaven on the children of man, to see if there are any who understand, who seek after God. [3] They have all turned aside; together they have become corrupt; there is none who does good, not even one.

Romans 3:9-12
[9] What then? Are we better than they? No, in no way. For we previously warned both Jews and Greeks that they are all under sin. [10] As it is written, "There is no one righteous; no, not one. [11] There is no one who understands. There is no one who seeks after God. [12] They have all turned away. They have together become unprofitable. There is no one who does good, no, not so much as one."

[12] * * *

Matthew 5:18-19
[18] For most certainly, I tell you, until heaven and earth pass away, not even one smallest letter (literally, iota) or one tiny pen stroke (or, serif) shall in any way pass away from the law, until all things are accomplished. [19] Therefore, whoever shall break one of these least commandments and teach others to do so, shall be called least in the Kingdom of Heaven; but whoever shall do and teach them shall be called great in the Kingdom of Heaven.

Matthew 12:36
36 I tell you that every idle word that men speak, they will give account of it in the day of judgment.

James 4:17
17 To him therefore who knows to do good, and doesn't do it, to him it is sin.

Isaiah 64:6
6 For we have all become like one who is unclean, and all our righteousness is like a polluted garment. We all fade like a leaf; and our iniquities, like the wind, take us away.

13 * * *
Proverbs 16:2 (ESV)
2 All the ways of a man are pure in his own eyes, but the LORD weighs the spirit.

Proverbs 21:2 (ESV)
2 Every way of a man is right in his own eyes, but the LORD weighs the heart.

14 * * *
Matthew 5:27-28
27 "You have heard that it was said, 'You shall not commit adultery; 28 but I tell you that everyone who gazes at a woman to lust after her has committed adultery with her already in his heart.

Matthew 15:18-20
18 But the things which proceed out of the mouth come out of the heart, and they defile the man. 19 For out of the heart come evil thoughts, murders, adulteries, sexual sins, thefts, false testimony, and blasphemies. 20 These are the things which defile the man; but to eat with unwashed hands doesn't defile the man."

15 * * *
James 3:6-8
6 And the tongue is a fire. The world of iniquity among our members is the tongue, which defiles the whole body, and sets on

fire the course of nature, and is set on fire by Gehenna. (or, Hell) [7] For every kind of animal, bird, creeping thing, and sea creature, is tamed, and has been tamed by mankind; [8] but nobody can tame the tongue. It is a restless evil, full of deadly poison.

Jeremiah 9:8-9 (ESV)
[8] Their tongue is a deadly arrow; it speaks deceitfully; with his mouth each speaks peace to his neighbor, but in his heart he plans an ambush for him. [9] Shall I not punish them for these things? declares the LORD, and shall I not avenge myself on a nation such as this?

16 * * *

Romans 2:5-11
[5] But according to your hardness and unrepentant heart you are treasuring up for yourself wrath in the day of wrath, revelation, and of the righteous judgment of God; [6] who "will pay back to everyone according to their works:" [7] to those who by perseverance in well-doing seek for glory, honor, and incorruptibility, eternal life; [8] but to those who are self-seeking, and don't obey the truth, but obey unrighteousness, will be wrath, indignation, [9] oppression, and anguish on every soul of man who does evil, to the Jew first, and also to the Greek. [10] But glory, honor, and peace go to every man who does good, to the Jew first, and also to the Greek. [11] For there is no partiality with God.

Romans 6:23
[23] For the wages of sin is death, but the free gift of God is eternal life in Christ Jesus our Lord.

17 * * *

Matthew 5:48
Therefore you shall be perfect, just as your Father in heaven is perfect.

Ephesians 5:1
Be therefore imitators of God, as beloved children.

18 * * *

Matthew 19:24-26
24 Again I tell you, it is easier for a camel to go through a needle's eye than for a rich man to enter into God's Kingdom." 25 When the disciples heard it, they were exceedingly astonished, saying, "Who then can be saved?" 26 Looking at them, Jesus said, "With men this is impossible, but with God all things are possible."

Luke 1:37
37 For nothing spoken by God is impossible. (or, "For everything spoken by God is possible.")

Chapter 5

STUBBORN REBELS

To many people it would seem like a gross impossibility that God would destroy what He created, yet that is exactly what He did. As previously noted, following man's original disobedience and separation from God, life became more difficult. Even so, man did propagate the earth as was God's intention. But more people resulted in more sin.

Humanity became so utterly polluted that God was extremely grieved with what He saw taking place on Earth. He deeply regretted that He had even created mankind![1] Consequently, He judged Earth's inhabitants by causing a massive flood that destroyed all living creatures with the exception of just eight people, plus the animals carried along with them on an ark.[2]

The man called Noah was determined by God to be righteous and blameless among his generation, though not sinless.[3] So, Noah, his wife, his three sons and their wives then became the starting point for repopulating the Earth.[4] This was a gracious provision made because of the great mercy of God and because of His perseverance in executing His long-term strategy for mankind.

Fractured Society

Yet again as the generations developed, the prideful insistence of man to exalt himself separately from God brought more judgment upon himself. The people planned to construct a tower to the heavens, known as the Tower of Babel, by which they would establish themselves, or make a name for themselves in the Earth. The intent of their hearts, just as it was (and still is) with Satan, was to lift themselves up above God, divorcing themselves from the very One who created them.

Up to this point they had one language, so God confused their language and scattered them into different territories.[5] Consequently, the goal of the devil to manipulate and prey upon the weakness of mankind, consolidating them against God, would become more difficult to accomplish. This was a loving response from the God who desires only the best for all His people. Any good father takes steps to discipline and guide the behaviors of his child, especially to protect his life; a characteristic which comes directly from being made in the image of the Father of all fathers.

Pending Fire

Mankind was given a fresh start; unfortunately, his inclination to be sinfully rebellious towards God has persisted throughout the ages. That is man's very nature, unless he gets a makeover from God. Ultimately God will judge the inhabitants of the earth again[6]; though in that day it will be as He promised, with fire and not with a flood[7]. The fact that God spared only eight people out of the entire population should give pause to everyone, especially those who prefer to believe that God is too loving to keep anyone away from Him for eternity.

Chapter 5 References:

1 * * *

Genesis 6:5-7 (ESV)
5 The LORD saw that the wickedness of man was great in the earth, and that every intention of the thoughts of his heart was only evil continually. 6 And the LORD regretted that he had made man on the earth, and it grieved him to his heart. 7 So the LORD said, "I will blot out man whom I have created from the face of the land, man and animals and creeping things and birds of the heavens, for I am sorry that I have made them."

2 * * *

Genesis 6:11-13
11 The earth was corrupt before God, and the earth was filled with violence. 12 God saw the earth, and saw that it was corrupt, for all flesh had corrupted their way on the earth. 13 God said to Noah, "I will bring an end to all flesh, for the earth is filled with violence through them. Behold, I will destroy them and the earth.

Genesis 6:17-18
17 I, even I, will bring the flood of waters on this earth, to destroy all flesh having the breath of life from under the sky. Everything that is in the earth will die. 18 But I will establish my covenant with you. You shall come into the ship, you, your sons, your wife, and your sons' wives with you.

3 * * *

Genesis 6:9
9 This is the history of the generations of Noah: Noah was a righteous man, blameless among the people of his time. Noah walked with God.

Genesis 7:1 (ESV)

---

¹ Then the LORD said to Noah, "Go into the ark, you and all your household, for I have seen that you are righteous before me in this generation.

4 * * *
Genesis 9:1
God blessed Noah and his sons, and said to them, "Be fruitful, multiply, and replenish the earth.

Genesis 9:18-19
¹⁸ The sons of Noah who went out from the ship were Shem, Ham, and Japheth. Ham is the father of Canaan. ¹⁹ These three were the sons of Noah, and from these the whole earth was populated.

5 * * *
Genesis 11:1-9 (ESV)
¹ Now the whole earth had one language and the same words. ² And as people migrated from the east, they found a plain in the land of Shinar and settled there. ³ And they said to one another, "Come, let us make bricks, and burn them thoroughly." And they had brick for stone, and bitumen for mortar. ⁴ Then they said, "Come, let us build ourselves a city and a tower with its top in the heavens, and let us make a name for ourselves, lest we be dispersed over the face of the whole earth." ⁵ And the LORD came down to see the city and the tower, which the children of man had built. ⁶ And the LORD said, "Behold, they are one people, and they have all one language, and this is only the beginning of what they will do. And nothing that they propose to do will now be impossible for them. ⁷ Come, let us go down and there confuse their language, so that they may not understand one another's speech." ⁸ So the LORD dispersed them from there over the face of all the earth, and they left off building the city. ⁹ Therefore its name was called Babel, because there the LORD confused the language of all the earth. And from there the LORD dispersed them over the face of all the earth.

6 * * *
Isaiah 34:1-4 (ESV)

---

[1] Draw near, O nations, to hear, and give attention, O peoples! Let the earth hear, and all that fills it; the world, and all that comes from it. [2] For the LORD is enraged against all the nations, and furious against all their host; he has devoted them to destruction, has given them over for slaughter. [3] Their slain shall be cast out, and the stench of their corpses shall rise; the mountains shall flow with their blood. [4] All the host of heaven shall rot away, and the skies roll up like a scroll. All their host shall fall, as leaves fall from the vine, like leaves falling from the fig tree.

Matthew 24:21
[21] for then there will be great suffering (or oppression), such as has not been from the beginning of the world until now, no, nor ever will be.

2 Peter 2:4-9
[4] For if God didn't spare angels when they sinned, but cast them down to Tartarus (Tartarus is another name for Hell), and committed them to pits of darkness to be reserved for judgment; [5] and didn't spare the ancient world, but preserved Noah with seven others, a preacher of righteousness, when he brought a flood on the world of the ungodly; [6] and turning the cities of Sodom and Gomorrah into ashes, condemned them to destruction, having made them an example to those who would live in an ungodly way; [7] and delivered righteous Lot, who was very distressed by the lustful life of the wicked [8] (for that righteous man dwelling among them was tormented in his righteous soul from day to day with seeing and hearing lawless deeds): [9] the Lord knows how to deliver the godly out of temptation and to keep the unrighteous under punishment for the day of judgment,

[7] * * *
Genesis 9:11-13
[11] I will establish my covenant with you: All flesh will not be cut off any more by the waters of the flood. There will never again be a flood to destroy the earth." [12] God said, "This is the token of the covenant which I make between me and you and every living creature that is with you, for perpetual generations: [13] I set my

rainbow in the cloud, and it will be a sign of a covenant between me and the earth.

2 Peter 3:3-12

3 knowing this first, that in the last days mockers will come, walking after their own lusts 4 and saying, "Where is the promise of his coming? For, from the day that the fathers fell asleep, all things continue as they were from the beginning of the creation." 5 For this they willfully forget that there were heavens from of old, and an earth formed out of water and amid water by the word of God, 6 by which means the world that existed then, being overflowed with water, perished. 7 But the heavens that exist now and the earth, by the same word have been stored up for fire, being reserved against the day of judgment and destruction of ungodly men. 8 But don't forget this one thing, beloved, that one day is with the Lord as a thousand years, and a thousand years as one day. 9 The Lord is not slow concerning his promise, as some count slowness; but he is patient with us, not wishing that anyone should perish, but that all should come to repentance. 10 But the day of the Lord will come as a thief in the night; in which the heavens will pass away with a great noise, and the elements will be dissolved with fervent heat, and the earth and the works that are in it will be burned up. 11 Therefore since all these things will be destroyed like this, what kind of people ought you to be in holy living and godliness, 12 looking for and earnestly desiring the coming of the day of God, which will cause the burning heavens to be dissolved, and the elements will melt with fervent heat?

Chapter 6

COSTLY RESISTANCE

To continue to facilitate His purposes on Earth, God singled out a man called Abram (which means *good father*), who He later renamed Abraham (which means *father of many nations*). In his life we again see God's desires revealed to promote the excellence of God and the purposes of God. Through Abram's family God would spiritually impact every nation on Earth.[1]

From Abram developed the Hebrew people, a branch of which eventually became the Israelite nation.[2] This people became enslaved in Egypt for many years, yet even during that oppression God blessed them greatly by multiplying their numbers.[3] Then God provided a leader for them in a man called Moses, who led them out from slavery through the miraculous power of God Himself.[4]

God set them apart to represent him on the Earth, divinely providing laws and guidelines by which they were to live their lives.[5] Through their obedience they would honor God by reflecting His goodness in the way they lived their lives. In so doing the Israelites also would show the rest of mankind the right way to live. Obedience would bring a great many blessings, but disobedience would bring a great many curses.[6]

A most important point to highlight here is that in spite of man's fallen condition, again it was God's intention to be directly involved with His chosen people. Initially, He made Israel into a nation without any man as a ruler, because He Himself wanted to be their ruler. All they had to do was to observe His guidelines and He would provide for their needs and protect them as well. But the Israelites wanted an earthly king so that they could be like the other nations. God answered favorably but reluctantly to their wishes; rejected from the close relationship He so desired.[7]

A World of Sin Pollutes God's Best

Time and again the Israelites failed in their appointed position, despite repeated guidance and warnings that God provided to them through His prophets. They were repeatedly lured into complicity with the sin of the world.[8] They formally observed the ritualistic practices of their religion, but their hearts were not for God.[9] Instead, they dishonored Him by turning to false gods and by disobeying His other commands also.[10]

As God promised, they were made to suffer for it.[11] At times an enemy nation was enabled by God to bring His judgment on Israel.[12] Nevertheless, every time the Israelites turned back to God, out of His great mercy and loving covenant with them, He welcomed them back with open arms.[13] To this day He has left open to them the same door to return to Him that is open to anyone else in the world, regardless of race or nationality or religion or sex or age or anything else.[14] In fact, the Jewish people still have a place in God's heart and God's plans.[15]

God Prevails Always

It is a precious, comforting and joyful thing to discover that these plans of God are not knee-jerk reactions on His part to the failures of man. That is just incredibly far from the truth. In fact, God has had a detailed plan to finally, completely and perfectly reconcile Israel, and all of mankind, to Himself, even before creation. And He laid out that plan in His Holy Bible. God knows the end of things from the very beginning, so He is not surprised when things do not go the way He would prefer them to go. It has been that way from the beginning of creation and will continue that way to the end of the history of man. He wrote the book, and things are happening just as He said they would. No matter how many times Israel, or mankind as a whole, has failed to follow through with God's desires, the plans of God have rolled on, and will continue to roll on, with certainty.

Many Prophecies Already Fulfilled

The following chapters will deal more specifically with God's solution to mankind's problem both for today and for the future as well, but many amazing details of God's plans can be found woven into the recorded history of Israel in the Bible. For example, going all the way back to the first work of the devil at the Fall of man in the Garden of Eden, God declared His intentions to bring forth a child, supernaturally born of a virgin, who ultimately would crush Satan.[16] This Person would come into the world through the line of Abraham, Isaac and Jacob; the final and eternal heir to the throne of Israel's King David.[17] This Person would be the One through whom would come the ultimate blessing for all nations as promised to Abraham.[18] This Person would be the prophesied Messiah (which means the Anointed One) of Israel, and the Savior of the entire world;[19] the One born in the town of Bethlehem and from the tribe of Judah.[20] All these things and much more about this individual were foretold from centuries past and came to fruition about 2000 years ago.[21] Regrettably, Israel failed to recognize and accept the coming of her Messiah, which resulted in Jerusalem being destroyed by the Romans.[22]

Man, Minus God, Equals Failure

The failure of the nation of Israel to fulfill all of God's purposes, up until today at least, further documents for us the woefully inadequate ability of mankind to overcome this world without God. As was previously presented, God created Adam and Eve to know Him and to love Him and to serve Him, but their choice to be independent brought sin and death into the world. The end result was the decimation of the human race, save for eight people. God singled out Noah and his family to be His representatives on Earth so that through them and their descendants the goodness of God would be manifested in the Earth. But again, evil permeated lives, and humanity was dispersed to form multiple nations. Even a cursory look back at those past events shows us that families, relationships and Godly living consistently can be seen at the heart of God's plans for humanity. His most excellent goodness and love is at the root of every step He has taken in the life of mankind in the past, and will be so in the future as well.

The biblical record, from beginning to end, reveals people and nations who succeeded when living in God's way, but failed when they put God aside and chose their own way instead. The weakness of man's fallen nature is preyed upon by spiritual forces of darkness, so that man is simply not able to correct the problem of sin and separation from God on his own. No amount of right living or good works can ever satisfy the perfect and righteous God.[23] That doesn't mean that we shouldn't bother doing such things, because we definitely should. It just means that such works alone are not adequate to lift us up to the standard of perfection necessary. A great many people before us have tried and failed; it is wise to learn from their mistake and find God's way of doing things instead. I use the singular word *mistake* because while there are many ways to offend God, the root of the problem is in thinking that it's possible to partially or totally ignore God's way, living a life of one's own choosing, and still be welcomed into God's presence when death comes knocking. The *essential spiritual truth* that this book is all about is the only way to avoid that mistake.

Chapter 6 References:

1 * * *

Genesis 18:17-19 (ESV)
[17] The LORD said, "Shall I hide from Abraham what I am about to do, [18] seeing that Abraham shall surely become a great and mighty nation, and all the nations of the earth shall be blessed in him? [19] For I have chosen him, that he may command his children and his household after him to keep the way of the LORD by doing righteousness and justice, so that the LORD may bring to Abraham what he has promised him."

Galatians 3:7-9
[7] Know therefore that those who are of faith are children of Abraham. [8] The Scripture, foreseeing that God would justify the Gentiles by faith, preached the Good News beforehand to Abraham, saying, "In you all the nations will be blessed." [9] So then, those who are of faith are blessed with the faithful Abraham.

2 * * *
Genesis 17:1-5 (ESV)

---

[1] When Abram was ninety-nine years old the LORD appeared to Abram and said to him, "I am God Almighty; walk before me, and be blameless, [2] that I may make my covenant between me and you, and may multiply you greatly." [3] Then Abram fell on his face. And God said to him, [4] "Behold, my covenant is with you, and you shall be the father of a multitude of nations. [5] No longer shall your name be called Abram, but your name shall be Abraham, for I have made you the father of a multitude of nations.

Genesis 21:1-3 (ESV)
[1] The LORD visited Sarah as he had said, and the LORD did to Sarah as he had promised. [2] And Sarah conceived and bore Abraham a son in his old age at the time of which God had spoken to him. [3] Abraham called the name of his son who was born to him, whom Sarah bore him, Isaac.

Genesis 25:24-26
[24] When her days to be delivered were fulfilled, behold, there were twins in her womb. [25] The first came out red all over, like a hairy garment. They named him Esau. [26] After that, his brother came out, and his hand had hold on Esau's heel. He was named Jacob. Isaac was sixty years old when she bore them.

Genesis 32:27-28
[27] He said to him, "What is your name?" He said, "Jacob". [28] He said, "Your name will no longer be called Jacob, but Israel; for you have fought with God and with men, and have prevailed."

[3] * * *
Exodus 1:7-14
[7] The children of Israel were fruitful, and increased abundantly, and multiplied, and grew exceedingly mighty; and the land was filled with them. [8] Now there arose a new king over Egypt, who didn't know Joseph. [9] He said to his people, "Behold, the people of the children of Israel are more and mightier than we. [10] Come, let's deal wisely with them, lest they multiply, and it happen that when any war breaks out, they also join themselves to our enemies and fight against us, and escape out of the land." [11] Therefore they set taskmasters over them to afflict them with their burdens. They

built storage cities for Pharaoh: Pithom and Raamses. [12] But the more they afflicted them, the more they multiplied and the more they spread out. They started to dread the children of Israel. [13] The Egyptians ruthlessly made the children of Israel serve, [14] and they made their lives bitter with hard service in mortar and in brick, and in all kinds of service in the field, all their service, in which they ruthlessly made them serve.

4 * * *

Exodus 3:7-10 (ESV)

[7] Then the LORD said, "I have surely seen the affliction of my people who are in Egypt and have heard their cry because of their taskmasters. I know their sufferings, [8] and I have come down to deliver them out of the hand of the Egyptians and to bring them up out of that land to a good and broad land, a land flowing with milk and honey, to the place of the Canaanites, the Hittites, the Amorites, the Perizzites, the Hivites, and the Jebusites. [9] And now, behold, the cry of the people of Israel has come to me, and I have also seen the oppression with which the Egyptians oppress them. [10] Come, I will send you to Pharaoh that you may bring my people, the children of Israel, out of Egypt."

Exodus 7:20-21 (ESV)

[20] Moses and Aaron did as the LORD commanded. In the sight of Pharaoh and in the sight of his servants he lifted up the staff and struck the water in the Nile, and all the water in the Nile turned into blood. [21] And the fish in the Nile died, and the Nile stank, so that the Egyptians could not drink water from the Nile. There was blood throughout all the land of Egypt.

Exodus 8:24 (ESV)

[24] And the LORD did so. There came great swarms of flies into the house of Pharaoh and into his servants' houses. Throughout all the land of Egypt the land was ruined by the swarms of flies.

5 * * *

Exodus 19:3-6 (ESV)

[3] while Moses went up to God. The LORD called to him out of the mountain, saying, "Thus you shall say to the house of Jacob, and

tell the people of Israel: 4 You yourselves have seen what I did to the Egyptians, and how I bore you on eagles' wings and brought you to myself. 5 Now therefore, if you will indeed obey my voice and keep my covenant, you shall be my treasured possession among all peoples, for all the earth is mine; 6 and you shall be to me a kingdom of priests and a holy nation. These are the words that you shall speak to the people of Israel."

Deuteronomy 7:7-10 (ESV)
7 It was not because you were more in number than any other people that the LORD set his love on you and chose you, for you were the fewest of all peoples, 8 but it is because the LORD loves you and is keeping the oath that he swore to your fathers, that the LORD has brought you out with a mighty hand and redeemed you from the house of slavery, from the hand of Pharaoh king of Egypt. 9 Know therefore that the LORD your God is God, the faithful God who keeps covenant and steadfast love with those who love him and keep his commandments, to a thousand generations, 10 and repays to their face those who hate him, by destroying them. He will not be slack with one who hates him. He will repay him to his face.

6 * * *

Deuteronomy 4:1, 6-8 (ESV)
1 "And now, O Israel, listen to the statutes and the rules that I am teaching you, and do them, that you may live, and go in and take possession of the land that the LORD, the God of your fathers, is giving you.
6 Keep them and do them, for that will be your wisdom and your understanding in the sight of the peoples, who, when they hear all these statutes, will say, 'Surely this great nation is a wise and understanding people.' 7 For what great nation is there that has a god so near to it as the LORD our God is to us, whenever we call upon him? 8 And what great nation is there, that has statutes and rules so righteous as all this law that I set before you today?

Deuteronomy 28:1-2, 15 (ESV)
1 "And if you faithfully obey the voice of the LORD your God, being careful to do all his commandments that I command you today,

68

the LORD your God will set you high above all the nations of the earth. 2 And all these blessings shall come upon you and overtake you, if you obey the voice of the LORD your God.

15 "But if you will not obey the voice of the LORD your God or be careful to do all his commandments and his statutes that I command you today, then all these curses shall come upon you and overtake you.

7 * * *

1 Samuel 8:4-7 (ESV)

4 Then all the elders of Israel gathered together and came to Samuel at Ramah 5 and said to him, "Behold, you are old and your sons do not walk in your ways. Now appoint for us a king to judge us like all the nations." 6 But the thing displeased Samuel when they said, "Give us a king to judge us." And Samuel prayed to the LORD. 7 And the LORD said to Samuel, "Obey the voice of the people in all that they say to you, for they have not rejected you, but they have rejected me from being king over them.

8 * * *

Isaiah 1:2-4 (ESV)

2 Hear, O heavens, and give ear, O earth; for the LORD has spoken: "Children have I reared and brought up, but they have rebelled against me. 3 The ox knows its owner, and the donkey its master's crib, but Israel does not know, my people do not understand." 4 Ah, sinful nation, a people laden with iniquity, offspring of evildoers, children who deal corruptly! They have forsaken the LORD, they have despised the Holy One of Israel, they are utterly estranged.

Jeremiah 7:23-28 (ESV)

23 But this command I gave them: 'Obey my voice, and I will be your God, and you shall be my people. And walk in all the way that I command you, that it may be well with you.' 24 But they did not obey or incline their ear, but walked in their own counsels and the stubbornness of their evil hearts, and went backward and not forward. 25 From the day that your fathers came out of the land of Egypt to this day, I have persistently sent all my servants the prophets to them, day after day. 26 Yet they did not listen to me or

incline their ear, but stiffened their neck. They did worse than their fathers. 27 "So you shall speak all these words to them, but they will not listen to you. You shall call to them, but they will not answer you. 28 And you shall say to them, 'This is the nation that did not obey the voice of the LORD their God, and did not accept discipline; truth has perished; it is cut off from their lips.

9 * * *
Isaiah 1:10-17 (ESV)
10 Hear the word of the LORD, you rulers of Sodom! Give ear to the teaching of our God, you people of Gomorrah! 11 "What to me is the multitude of your sacrifices? says the LORD; I have had enough of burnt offerings of rams and the fat of well-fed beasts; I do not delight in the blood of bulls, or of lambs, or of goats. 12 "When you come to appear before me, who has required of you this trampling of my courts? 13 Bring no more vain offerings; incense is an abomination to me. New moon and Sabbath and the calling of convocations— I cannot endure iniquity and solemn assembly. 14 Your new moons and your appointed feasts my soul hates; they have become a burden to me; I am weary of bearing them. 15 When you spread out your hands, I will hide my eyes from you; even though you make many prayers, I will not listen; your hands are full of blood. 16 Wash yourselves; make yourselves clean; remove the evil of your deeds from before my eyes; cease to do evil, 17 learn to do good; seek justice, correct oppression; bring justice to the fatherless, plead the widow's cause.

Isaiah 29:13-14
13 The Lord said, "Because this people draws near with their mouth and honors me with their lips, but they have removed their heart far from me, and their fear of me is a commandment of men which has been taught; 14 therefore, behold, I will proceed to do a marvelous work among this people, even a marvelous work and a wonder; and the wisdom of their wise men will perish, and the understanding of their prudent men will be hidden."

10 * * *
Jeremiah 9:3-6 (ESV)

3 They bend their tongue like a bow; falsehood and not truth has grown strong in the land; for they proceed from evil to evil, and they do not know me, declares the LORD. 4 Let everyone beware of his neighbor, and put no trust in any brother, for every brother is a deceiver, and every neighbor goes about as a slanderer. 5 Everyone deceives his neighbor, and no one speaks the truth; they have taught their tongue to speak lies; they weary themselves committing iniquity. 6 Heaping oppression upon oppression, and deceit upon deceit, they refuse to know me, declares the LORD.

Jeremiah 16:10-13 (ESV)
10 "And when you tell this people all these words, and they say to you, 'Why has the LORD pronounced all this great evil against us? What is our iniquity? What is the sin that we have committed against the LORD our God?' 11 then you shall say to them: 'Because your fathers have forsaken me, declares the LORD, and have gone after other gods and have served and worshiped them, and have forsaken me and have not kept my law, 12 and because you have done worse than your fathers, for behold, every one of you follows his stubborn, evil will, refusing to listen to me. 13 Therefore I will hurl you out of this land into a land that neither you nor your fathers have known, and there you shall serve other gods day and night, for I will show you no favor.'

11 * * *
Daniel 9:8-14 (ESV)
8 To us, O LORD, belongs open shame, to our kings, to our princes, and to our fathers, because we have sinned against you. 9 To the Lord our God belong mercy and forgiveness, for we have rebelled against him 10 and have not obeyed the voice of the LORD our God by walking in his laws, which he set before us by his servants the prophets. 11 All Israel has transgressed your law and turned aside, refusing to obey your voice. And the curse and oath that are written in the Law of Moses the servant of God have been poured out upon us, because we have sinned against him. 12 He has confirmed his words, which he spoke against us and against our rulers who ruled us, by bringing upon us a great calamity. For under the whole heaven there has not been done anything like what has been done against Jerusalem. 13 As it is written in the

Law of Moses, all this calamity has come upon us; yet we have not entreated the favor of the LORD our God, turning from our iniquities and gaining insight by your truth. [14] Therefore the LORD has kept ready the calamity and has brought it upon us, for the LORD our God is righteous in all the works that he has done, and we have not obeyed his voice.

[12] * * *

Judges 2:12-15 (ESV)
[12] And they abandoned the LORD, the God of their fathers, who had brought them out of the land of Egypt. They went after other gods, from among the gods of the peoples who were around them, and bowed down to them. And they provoked the LORD to anger. [13] They abandoned the LORD and served the Baals and the Ashtaroth. [14] So the anger of the LORD was kindled against Israel, and he gave them over to plunderers, who plundered them. And he sold them into the hand of their surrounding enemies, so that they could no longer withstand their enemies. [15] Whenever they marched out, the hand of the LORD was against them for harm, as the LORD had warned, and as the LORD had sworn to them. And they were in terrible distress.

Jeremiah 25:8-11 (ESV)
[8] "Therefore thus says the LORD of hosts: Because you have not obeyed my words, [9] behold, I will send for all the tribes of the north, declares the LORD, and for Nebuchadnezzar the king of Babylon, my servant, and I will bring them against this land and its inhabitants, and against all these surrounding nations. I will devote them to destruction, and make them a horror, a hissing, and an everlasting desolation. [10] Moreover, I will banish from them the voice of mirth and the voice of gladness, the voice of the bridegroom and the voice of the bride, the grinding of the millstones and the light of the lamp. [11] This whole land shall become a ruin and a waste, and these nations shall serve the king of Babylon seventy years.

[13] * * *
Judges 3:7-9 (ESV)

7 And the people of Israel did what was evil in the sight of the LORD. They forgot the LORD their God and served the Baals and the Asheroth. 8 Therefore the anger of the LORD was kindled against Israel, and he sold them into the hand of Cushan-rishathaim king of Mesopotamia. And the people of Israel served Cushan-rishathaim eight years. 9 But when the people of Israel cried out to the LORD, the LORD raised up a deliverer for the people of Israel, who saved them, Othniel the son of Kenaz, Caleb's younger brother.

Judges 3:12-15 (ESV)
12 And the people of Israel again did what was evil in the sight of the LORD, and the LORD strengthened Eglon the king of Moab against Israel, because they had done what was evil in the sight of the LORD. 13 He gathered to himself the Ammonites and the Amalekites, and went and defeated Israel. And they took possession of the city of palms. 14 And the people of Israel served Eglon the king of Moab eighteen years. 15 Then the people of Israel cried out to the LORD, and the LORD raised up for them a deliverer, Ehud, the son of Gera, the Benjaminite, a left-handed man. The people of Israel sent tribute by him to Eglon the king of Moab.

Judges 4:1-3 (ESV)
1 And the people of Israel again did what was evil in the sight of the LORD after Ehud died. 2 And the LORD sold them into the hand of Jabin king of Canaan, who reigned in Hazor. The commander of his army was Sisera, who lived in Harosheth-hagoyim. 3 Then the people of Israel cried out to the LORD for help, for he had 900 chariots of iron and he oppressed the people of Israel cruelly for twenty years.

14 * * *

Hosea 14:1-2 (ESV)
1 Return, O Israel, to the LORD your God, for you have stumbled because of your iniquity. 2 Take with you words and return to the LORD; say to him, "Take away all iniquity; accept what is good, and we will pay with bulls the vows of our lips.

Romans 11:25-32
25 For I don't desire you to be ignorant, brothers (The word for "brothers" here and where context allows may also be correctly translated "brothers and sisters" or "siblings."), of this mystery, so that you won't be wise in your own conceits, that a partial hardening has happened to Israel, until the fullness of the Gentiles has come in, 26 and so all Israel will be saved. Even as it is written, "There will come out of Zion the Deliverer, and he will turn away ungodliness from Jacob. 27 This is my covenant with them, when I will take away their sins." 28 Concerning the Good News, they are enemies for your sake. But concerning the election, they are beloved for the fathers' sake. 29 For the gifts and the calling of God are irrevocable. 30 For as you in time past were disobedient to God, but now have obtained mercy by their disobedience, 31 even so these also have now been disobedient, that by the mercy shown to you they may also obtain mercy. 32 For God has bound all to disobedience, that he might have mercy on all.

15 * * *
Isaiah 54:7-10 (ESV)
7 For a brief moment I deserted you, but with great compassion I will gather you. 8 In overflowing anger for a moment I hid my face from you, but with everlasting love I will have compassion on you," says the LORD, your Redeemer. 9 "This is like the days of Noah to me: as I swore that the waters of Noah should no more go over the earth, so I have sworn that I will not be angry with you, and will not rebuke you. 10 For the mountains may depart and the hills be removed, but my steadfast love shall not depart from you, and my covenant of peace shall not be removed," says the LORD, who has compassion on you.

Jeremiah 31:31-33 (ESV)
31 "Behold, the days are coming, declares the LORD, when I will make a new covenant with the house of Israel and the house of Judah, 32 not like the covenant that I made with their fathers on the day when I took them by the hand to bring them out of the land of Egypt, my covenant that they broke, though I was their husband, declares the LORD. 33 For this is the covenant that I will make with the house of Israel after those days, declares the LORD:

I will put my law within them, and I will write it on their hearts. And I will be their God, and they shall be my people.

16 * * *

Genesis 3:15
15 I will put hostility between you and the woman, and between your offspring and her offspring. He will bruise your head, and you will bruise his heel."

Isaiah 7:14
14 Therefore the Lord himself will give you a sign. Behold, the virgin will conceive, and bear a son, and shall call his name Immanuel. ("Immanuel" means "God with us".)

Isaiah 9:6-7 (ESV)
6 For to us a child is born, to us a son is given; and the government shall be upon his shoulder, and his name shall be called Wonderful Counselor, Mighty God, Everlasting Father, Prince of Peace. 7 Of the increase of his government and of peace there will be no end, on the throne of David and over his kingdom, to establish it and to uphold it with justice and with righteousness from this time forth and forevermore. The zeal of the LORD of hosts will do this.

Matthew 1:18
18 Now the birth of Jesus Christ was like this: After his mother, Mary, was engaged to Joseph, before they came together, she was found pregnant by the Holy Spirit.

17 * * *

Isaiah 11:1-5 (ESV)
1 There shall come forth a shoot from the stump of Jesse, and a branch from his roots shall bear fruit. 2 And the Spirit of the LORD shall rest upon him, the Spirit of wisdom and understanding, the Spirit of counsel and might, the Spirit of knowledge and the fear of the LORD. 3 And his delight shall be in the fear of the LORD. He shall not judge by what his eyes see, or decide disputes by what his ears hear, 4 but with righteousness he shall judge the poor, and decide with equity for the meek of the earth; and he shall strike the earth with the rod of his mouth, and with the breath of his lips

he shall kill the wicked. ⁵ Righteousness shall be the belt of his waist, and faithfulness the belt of his loins.

Matthew 1:1-2
The book of the genealogy of Jesus Christ (Messiah (Hebrew) and Christ (Greek) both mean "Anointed One"), the son of David, the son of Abraham. ²Abraham became the father of Isaac. Isaac became the father of Jacob. Jacob became the father of Judah and his brothers.

Matthew 1:6
⁶ Jesse became the father of King David. David became the father of Solomon by her who had been Uriah's wife.

Matthew 1:16
¹⁶ Jacob became the father of Joseph, the husband of Mary, from whom was born Jesus ("Jesus" means "Salvation".), who is called Christ.

18 * * *

Genesis 26:3-5
³ Live in this land, and I will be with you, and will bless you. For I will give to you, and to your offspring, all these lands, and I will establish the oath which I swore to Abraham your father. ⁴ I will multiply your offspring as the stars of the sky, and will give all these lands to your offspring. In your offspring all the nations of the earth will be blessed, ⁵ because Abraham obeyed my voice, and kept my requirements, my commandments, my statutes, and my laws."

Isaiah 42:5-7 (ESV)
⁵ Thus says God, the LORD, who created the heavens and stretched them out, who spread out the earth and what comes from it, who gives breath to the people on it and spirit to those who walk in it: ⁶ "I am the LORD; I have called you in righteousness; I will take you by the hand and keep you; I will give you as a covenant for the people, a light for the nations, ⁷ to open the eyes that are blind, to bring out the prisoners from the dungeon, from the prison those who sit in darkness.

Jeremiah 23:5-6 (ESV)
5 "Behold, the days are coming, declares the LORD, when I will raise up for David a righteous Branch, and he shall reign as king and deal wisely, and shall execute justice and righteousness in the land. 6 In his days Judah will be saved, and Israel will dwell securely. And this is the name by which he will be called: 'The LORD is our righteousness.'

19 * * *

John 1:41-42
41 He first found his own brother, Simon, and said to him, "We have found the Messiah!" (which is, being interpreted, Christ; "Messiah" (Hebrew) and "Christ" (Greek) both mean "Anointed One".). 42 He brought him to Jesus. Jesus looked at him, and said, "You are Simon the son of Jonah. You shall be called Cephas" (which is by interpretation, Peter; "Cephas" (Aramaic) and "Peter" (Greek) both mean "Rock".).

Acts 4:24-28
24 When they heard it, they lifted up their voice to God with one accord, and said, "O Lord, you are God, who made the heaven, the earth, the sea, and all that is in them; 25 who by the mouth of your servant, David, said, 'Why do the nations rage, and the peoples plot a vain thing? 26 The kings of the earth take a stand, and the rulers take council together, against the Lord, and against his Christ.' 27 "For truly, both Herod and Pontius Pilate, with the Gentiles and the people of Israel, were gathered together against your holy servant, Jesus, whom you anointed, 28 to do whatever your hand and your council foreordained to happen.

John 4:42
42 They said to the woman, "Now we believe, not because of your speaking; for we have heard for ourselves, and know that this is indeed the Christ, the Savior of the world."

1 Timothy 4:10

---

[10] For to this end we both labor and suffer reproach, because we have set our trust in the living God, who is the Savior of all men, especially of those who believe.

20 * * *

Genesis 49:10
[10] The scepter will not depart from Judah, nor the ruler's staff from between his feet,
until he comes to whom it belongs. The obedience of the peoples will be to him.

Micah 5:2
[2] But you, Bethlehem Ephrathah, being small among the clans of Judah, out of you one will come out to me that is to be ruler in Israel; whose goings out are from of old, from ancient times.

Matthew 2:1
Now when Jesus was born in Bethlehem of Judea in the days of King Herod, behold, wise men (The word for "wise men" (magoi) can also mean teachers, scientists, physicians, astrologers, seers, interpreters of dreams, or sorcerers.) from the east came to Jerusalem, saying,

Luke 2:4-5
[4] Joseph also went up from Galilee, out of the city of Nazareth, into Judea, to David's city, which is called Bethlehem, because he was of the house and family of David; [5] to enroll himself with Mary, who was pledged to be married to him as wife, being pregnant.

21 * * *

John 1:14
[14] The Word became flesh, and lived among us. We saw his glory, such glory as of the one and only Son of the Father, full of grace and truth.

1 John 1:1-3
That which was from the beginning, that which we have heard, that which we have seen with our eyes, that which we saw, and our hands touched, concerning the Word of life [2] (and the life was

revealed, and we have seen, and testify, and declare to you the life, the eternal life, which was with the Father, and was revealed to us); 3 that which we have seen and heard we declare to you, that you also may have fellowship with us. Yes, and our fellowship is with the Father, and with his Son, Jesus Christ.

22 * * *

John 1:10-11

10 He was in the world, and the world was made through him, and the world didn't recognize him. 11 He came to his own, and those who were his own didn't receive him.

Luke 19:41-44

41 When he came near, he saw the city and wept over it, 42 saying, "If you, even you, had known today the things which belong to your peace! But now, they are hidden from your eyes. 43 For the days will come on you, when your enemies will throw up a barricade against you, surround you, hem you in on every side, 44 and will dash you and your children within you to the ground. They will not leave in you one stone on another, because you didn't know the time of your visitation."

23 * * *

Galatians 2:16

16 yet knowing that a man is not justified by the works of the law but through faith in Jesus Christ, even we believed in Christ Jesus, that we might be justified by faith in Christ, and not by the works of the law, because no flesh will be justified by the works of the law.

Galatians 3:10-11

10 For as many as are of the works of the law are under a curse. For it is written, "Cursed is everyone who doesn't continue in all things that are written in the book of the law, to do them." 11 Now that no man is justified by the law before God is evident, for, "The righteous will live by faith."

Chapter 7

SPIRITUAL RESTORATION

Before looking at what God has done to bridge the chasm between Himself and all people, let's first refocus on the nature and scope of mankind's predicament. To begin with, from conception man exists in a lower state of being than originally created by God. A spiritual disconnect exists because the ongoing presence of sin requires separation. Even the simplest of sins is detestable to the perfect God of creation.

The first sin was instigated by Satan, and he and all those who serve him persist in their efforts daily wherever they can get their foot in the door. Consequently, man must struggle with a weak and sinful nature even if he were left alone, but that difficulty is only compounded by a host of evil beings who strive to make matters worse. Then there is the reality that man does not have the capability to compensate for his sins on his own to restore his broken relationship with God. No matter how "good" one tries to be or no matter how many "good deeds" one does in his lifetime, it all falls far short of the perfection required to be reconciled to God. So, man simply has no way on his own to avoid spiritual death, which is separation from God for eternity.

God Paid the Price of Justice

But God has the perfect solution to that problem, one which He had already planned even before the creation.[1] His heart's desire is to have a close and personal relationship with each and every person, yet because He is a perfectly just God, He must still require that every sin be paid for.[2] Since the price for sin is death[3], God's solution was to pay the price Himself. To make things right again, restoring the broken relationship with His human creation, God would die on behalf of mankind.

Overview of the Trinity

Before going further on this subject, a very brief overview of the personhood of God will be helpful. There are three persons of God, yet one God. This is a reality widely known to many people though it's probably safe to say, not completely understood by anyone. The three persons of God are the Father, the Son who is Jesus Christ, and the Holy Spirit. They are separate, all equally God, and they totally, completely and beautifully work together as One.[4] The existence of the Trinity is well attested to in the Scriptures, where among other things: the Father is seen as the Supreme One over all things and the One who sent His Son to reveal Himself to man;[5] Jesus is seen as the One who reconciled mankind to God and is King over the Earth;[6] and the Holy Spirit is seen as the One who is presently on Earth completing God's plans.[7] Rest in the knowledge that most people have difficulty comprehending the Trinity, so don't be overly concerned at this point. If you follow this book to its point of conclusion and ultimately find yourself reconciled to God by His great mercy, He will give you better insight, understanding and appreciation for its reality.[8]

How Jesus Paid the Price

Now getting back to the problem of sin and God's solution to the problem, the Father sent His only son, Jesus, the Christ (which means the Anointed One; that is, the Jewish Messiah), to suffer and die on behalf of mankind.[9] Jesus was God and yet also man, as He came into the world as a baby.[10] As was prophesied long before His birth though, Jesus was divinely and supernaturally conceived so that His life was not even blemished with the fallen condition that came to all men through Adam and Eve's failure.[11] Then He grew to manhood without committing any sin at all, so He was the only one qualified to be the perfect sacrifice that would meet the standard required by the God of perfection.[12]

Throughout His earthly life Jesus destroyed the works of the devil by overcoming every temptation to sin that could be thrown at any man. Consequently, Satan stands judged even though God has chosen to allow him to remain free to operate into the last days.[13] His most evil efforts will only serve to accomplish the purposes of God.

When the time was right, Jesus willingly took upon Himself, on a cross, every sin of mankind that had already been committed, along with those that would be committed in the future.[14] To put it in the legal sense in which it was done, the punishment required and the cost to be paid for all of mankind's crimes was paid for by Jesus. He paid the penalty that no man could possibly pay, substituting His own sinless life for ours and redeeming man from the grip of death. Jesus died our spiritual death for us and so the wrath of God for mankind's sin was completely and forever satisfied.[15] The Supreme Judge has made His final decision; the price for sin has been paid in full, and anyone who has the sincere desire is welcome to participate in the outcome.

The Gift of Eternal Life -
Just Waiting to be Received

Looking back to the Israelites, a similar decision had to be made by every Hebrew family just prior to their being set free from slavery in Egypt. At that time, they were required by God to sacrifice an unblemished lamb and apply its blood to the doorframe of their homes. In doing so, that home would be protected from the last and greatest judgment about to come upon the whole nation of Egypt: the taking of the life of every first-born son, including the first-born of the animals.[16] This was a foreshadowing of how Jesus' blood would be poured out centuries later as a protection for His people, so Jesus is known also as "The Lamb of God".

The Father sacrificed His perfect Son to save mankind from the judgment of eternal death.[17] But following Jesus' death and burial came His bodily resurrection and glorious ascension back into heaven, where He is now seated at the right hand of God.[18] Because Jesus overcame death by His own sinless life[19], anyone who puts their trust in Him, believing by faith in Jesus' full payment for sin, can also look forward to being resurrected to life.[20] The time is coming when all who have died will be resurrected, some to eternal life but the others to eternal death.[21] Therefore, though we still face physical death in our mortal bodies, we now have the opportunity to live forever with God in a new eternal body, if we so choose.[22]

Chapter 7 References:

₁ * * *

Romans 1:1-4
Paul, a servant of Jesus Christ, called to be an apostle, set apart for the Good News of God, 2 which he promised before through his prophets in the holy Scriptures, 3 concerning his Son, who was born of the offspring (or, seed) of David according to the flesh, 4 who was declared to be the Son of God with power, according to the Spirit of holiness, by the resurrection from the dead, Jesus Christ our Lord,

Romans 14:24-26
24 Now to him who is able to establish you according to my Good News and the preaching of Jesus Christ, according to the revelation of the mystery which has been kept secret through long ages, 25 but now is revealed, and by the Scriptures of the prophets, according to the commandment of the eternal God, is made known for obedience of faith to all the nations; 26 to the only wise God, through Jesus Christ, to whom be the glory forever! Amen. (Some translations place these verses as Romans 16:25-27)

1 Corinthians 2:7
7 But we speak God's wisdom in a mystery, the wisdom that has been hidden, which God foreordained before the worlds for our glory,

₂ * * *

John 14:20-21
20 In that day you will know that I am in my Father, and you in me, and I in you. 21 One who has my commandments and keeps them, that person is one who loves me. One who loves me will be loved by my Father, and I will love him, and will reveal myself to him."

Romans 5:10
10 For if while we were enemies, we were reconciled to God through the death of his Son, much more, being reconciled, we will be saved by his life.

Psalm 89:14

Righteousness and justice are the foundation of your throne. Loving kindness and truth go before your face.

2 Chronicles 19:7 (ESV)
7 Now then, let the fear of the LORD be upon you. Be careful what you do, for there is no injustice with the LORD our God, or partiality or taking bribes."

3 * * *
Romans 5:12
Therefore as sin entered into the world through one man, and death through sin; so death passed to all men, because all sinned.

Romans 6:23
For the wages of sin is death, but the free gift of God is eternal life in Christ Jesus our Lord.

4 * * *
Matthew 3:13-17
13 Then Jesus came from Galilee to the Jordan (i.e. the Jordan River) to John, to be baptized by him. 14 But John would have hindered him, saying, "I need to be baptized by you, and you come to me?" 15 But Jesus, answering, said to him, "Allow it now, for this is the fitting way for us to fulfill all righteousness." Then he allowed him. 16 Jesus, when he was baptized, went up directly from the water: and behold, the heavens were opened to him. He saw the Spirit of God descending as a dove, and coming on him. 17 Behold, a voice out of the heavens said, "This is my beloved Son, with whom I am well pleased."

1 Peter 1:2
 according to the foreknowledge of God the Father, in sanctification of the Spirit, that you may obey Jesus Christ and be sprinkled with his blood: Grace to you and peace be multiplied.

5 * * *
John 3:16

For God so loved the world, that he gave his one and only Son, that whoever believes in him should not perish, but have eternal life.

1 Corinthians 11:3
But I would have you know that the head (or, origin) of every man is Christ, and the head (or, origin) of the woman is man, and the head (or, origin) of Christ is God.

1 Corinthians 15:22-28
22 For as in Adam all die, so also in Christ all will be made alive. 23 But each in his own order: Christ the first fruits, then those who are Christ's, at his coming. 24 Then the end comes, when he will deliver up the Kingdom to God, even the Father, when he will have abolished all rule and all authority and power. 25 For he must reign until he has put all his enemies under his feet. 26 The last enemy that will be abolished is death. 27 For, "He put all things in subjection under his feet." But when he says, "All things are put in subjection", it is evident that he is excepted who subjected all things to him. 28 When all things have been subjected to him, then the Son will also himself be subjected to him who subjected all things to him, that God may be all in all.

6 * * *

John 14:6
Jesus said to him, "I am the way, the truth, and the life. No one comes to the Father, except through me.

Daniel 7:13-14
13 "I saw in the night visions, and behold, there came with the clouds of the sky one like a son of man, and he came even to the ancient of days, and they brought him near before him. 14 Dominion was given him, and glory, and a kingdom, that all the peoples, nations, and languages should serve him. His dominion is an everlasting dominion, which will not pass away, and his kingdom one that which will not be destroyed.

Revelation 19:13-16

[13] He is clothed in a garment sprinkled with blood. His name is called "The Word of God." [14] The armies which are in heaven followed him on white horses, clothed in white, pure, fine linen. [15] Out of his mouth proceeds a sharp, double-edged sword, that with it he should strike the nations. He will rule them with an iron rod. He treads the wine press of the fierceness of the wrath of God, the Almighty. [16] He has on his garment and on his thigh a name written, "KING OF KINGS, AND LORD OF LORDS."

7 * * *

John 14:16-17
[16] I will pray to the Father, and he will give you another Counselor (Greek Parakletos: Counselor, Helper, Advocate, Intercessor, and Comforter), that he may be with you forever: [17] the Spirit of truth, whom the world can't receive; for it doesn't see him and doesn't know him. You know him, for he lives with you, and will be in you.

John 15:26-27
[26] "When the Counselor (Greek Parakletos: Counselor, Helper, Advocate, Intercessor, and Comforter) has come, whom I will send to you from the Father, the Spirit of truth, who proceeds from the Father, he will testify about me. [27] You will also testify, because you have been with me from the beginning.

8 * * *

Zechariah 4:6 (ESV)
[6] Then he said to me, "This is the word of the LORD to Zerubbabel: Not by might, nor by power, but by my Spirit, says the LORD of hosts.

2 Corinthians 13:14
The grace of the Lord Jesus Christ, God's love, and the fellowship of the Holy Spirit be with you all. Amen.

Titus 3:4-6
[4] But when the kindness of God our Savior and his love toward mankind appeared, [5] not by works of righteousness which we did ourselves, but according to his mercy, he saved us through the

washing of regeneration and renewing by the Holy Spirit, 6 whom he poured out on us richly, through Jesus Christ our Savior;

9 * * *

John 6:38-40
38 For I have come down from heaven, not to do my own will, but the will of him who sent me. 39 This is the will of my Father who sent me, that of all he has given to me I should lose nothing, but should raise him up at the last day. 40 This is the will of the one who sent me, that everyone who sees the Son, and believes in him, should have eternal life; and I will raise him up at the last day."

John 8:42
Therefore Jesus said to them, "If God were your father, you would love me, for I came out and have come from God. For I haven't come of myself, but he sent me.

Acts 2:21-23
21 It will be that whoever will call on the name of the Lord will be saved.' 22 "Men of Israel, hear these words! Jesus of Nazareth, a man approved by God to you by mighty works and wonders and signs which God did by him among you, even as you yourselves know, 23 him, being delivered up by the determined counsel and foreknowledge of God, you have taken by the hand of lawless men, crucified and killed;

10 * * *

Matthew 1:18-25
18 Now the birth of Jesus Christ was like this: After his mother, Mary, was engaged to Joseph, before they came together, she was found pregnant by the Holy Spirit. 19 Joseph, her husband, being a righteous man, and not willing to make her a public example, intended to put her away secretly. 20 But when he thought about these things, behold, an angel of the Lord appeared to him in a dream, saying, "Joseph, son of David, don't be afraid to take to yourself Mary as your wife, for that which is conceived in her is of the Holy Spirit. 21 She shall give birth to a son. You shall name him Jesus ("Jesus" means Salvation.), for it is he who shall save his people from their sins." 22 Now all this has happened that it might

be fulfilled which was spoken by the Lord through the prophet, saying, 23 "Behold, the virgin shall be with child, and shall give birth to a son. They shall call his name Immanuel," which is, being interpreted, "God with us." 24 Joseph arose from his sleep, and did as the angel of the Lord commanded him, and took his wife to himself; 25 and didn't know her sexually until she had given birth to her firstborn son. He named him Jesus.

Galatians 4:4-5
4 But when the fullness of the time came, God sent out his Son, born to a woman, born under the law, 5 that he might redeem those who were under the law, that we might receive the adoption as children.

1 Timothy 3:16
Without controversy, the mystery of godliness is great: God was revealed in the flesh, justified in the spirit, seen by angels, preached among the nations, believed on in the world, and received up in glory.

11 * * *

Isaiah 7:14
Therefore the Lord himself will give you a sign. Behold, the virgin will conceive, and bear a son, and shall call his name Immanuel. ("Immanuel" means "God with us".)

Isaiah 53:7
He was oppressed, yet when he was afflicted he didn't open his mouth. As a lamb that is led to the slaughter, and as a sheep that before its shearers is silent, so he didn't open his mouth.

1 Peter 1:17-19
17 If you call on him as Father, who without respect of persons judges according to each man's work, pass the time of your living as foreigners here in reverent fear, 18 knowing that you were redeemed, not with corruptible things, with silver or gold, from the useless way of life handed down from your fathers, 19 but with precious blood, as of a lamb without blemish or spot, the blood of Christ,

---

12 * * *

2 Corinthians 5:21
For him who knew no sin he made to be sin on our behalf; so that in him we might become the righteousness of God.

Hebrews 4:15
For we don't have a high priest who can't be touched with the feeling of our infirmities, but one who has been in all points tempted like we are, yet without sin.

13 * * *

John 12:31
Now is the judgment of this world. Now the prince of this world will be cast out.

John 16:11
about judgment, because the prince of this world has been judged.

1 John 3:8
He who sins is of the devil, for the devil has been sinning from the beginning. To this end the Son of God was revealed: that he might destroy the works of the devil.

14 * * *

John 10:17-18
[17] Therefore the Father loves me, because I lay down my life, that I may take it again. [18] No one takes it away from me, but I lay it down by myself. I have power to lay it down, and I have power to take it again. I received this commandment from my Father."

Romans 5:18-19
[18] So then as through one trespass, all men were condemned; even so through one act of righteousness, all men were justified to life. [19] For as through the one man's disobedience many were made sinners, even so through the obedience of the one, many will be made righteous.

1 Corinthians 15:3-4 _____

3 For I delivered to you first of all that which I also received: that Christ died for our sins according to the Scriptures, 4 that he was buried, that he was raised on the third day according to the Scriptures,

Hebrews 10:10
by which will we have been sanctified through the offering of the body of Jesus Christ once for all.

1 Peter 2:24
He himself bore our sins in his body on the tree, that we, having died to sins, might live to righteousness. You were healed by his wounds. (or, stripes)

15 * * *
John 3:36
One who believes in the Son has eternal life, but one who disobeys (the same word can be translated "disobeys" or "disbelieves" in this context.) the Son won't see life, but the wrath of God remains on him."

1 John 2:2
And he is the atoning sacrifice for our sins, and not for ours only, but also for the whole world.

Hebrews 10:12
but he, when he had offered one sacrifice for sins forever, sat down on the right hand of God,

Mark 10:45
For the Son of Man also came not to be served, but to serve, and to give his life as a ransom for many."

16 * * *
Exodus 11:4-5 (ESV)
4 So Moses said, "Thus says the LORD: 'About midnight I will go out in the midst of Egypt, 5 and every firstborn in the land of Egypt shall die, from the firstborn of Pharaoh who sits on his throne,

---

even to the firstborn of the slave girl who is behind the handmill, and all the firstborn of the cattle.

Exodus 12:3-7, 11-13 (ESV)

3 Tell all the congregation of Israel that on the tenth day of this month every man shall take a lamb according to their fathers' houses, a lamb for a household. 4 And if the household is too small for a lamb, then he and his nearest neighbor shall take according to the number of persons; according to what each can eat you shall make your count for the lamb. 5 Your lamb shall be without blemish, a male a year old. You may take it from the sheep or from the goats, 6 and you shall keep it until the fourteenth day of this month, when the whole assembly of the congregation of Israel shall kill their lambs at twilight. 7 "Then they shall take some of the blood and put it on the two doorposts and the lintel of the houses in which they eat it.

11 In this manner you shall eat it: with your belt fastened, your sandals on your feet, and your staff in your hand. And you shall eat it in haste. It is the LORD's Passover. 12 For I will pass through the land of Egypt that night, and I will strike all the firstborn in the land of Egypt, both man and beast; and on all the gods of Egypt I will execute judgments: I am the LORD. 13 The blood shall be a sign for you, on the houses where you are. And when I see the blood, I will pass over you, and no plague will befall you to destroy you, when I strike the land of Egypt.

17 * * *

Isaiah 53:10 (ESV)

10 Yet it was the will of the LORD to crush him; he has put him to grief; when his soul makes an offering for guilt, he shall see his offspring; he shall prolong his days; the will of the LORD shall prosper in his hand.

John 1:29

The next day, he saw Jesus coming to him, and said, "Behold, the Lamb of God, who takes away the sin of the world!

1 Corinthians 5:7

Purge out the old yeast, that you may be a new lump, even as you are unleavened. For indeed Christ, our Passover, has been sacrificed in our place.

Revelation 7:17
for the Lamb who is in the middle of the throne shepherds them and leads them to springs of life-giving waters. And God will wipe away every tear from their eyes."

18 * * *
Mark 9:31
For he was teaching his disciples, and said to them, "The Son of Man is being handed over to the hands of men, and they will kill him; and when he is killed, on the third day he will rise again."

Matthew 28:1-7
Now after the Sabbath, as it began to dawn on the first day of the week, Mary Magdalene and the other Mary came to see the tomb. 2 Behold, there was a great earthquake, for an angel of the Lord descended from the sky and came and rolled away the stone from the door and sat on it. 3 His appearance was like lightning, and his clothing white as snow. 4 For fear of him, the guards shook, and became like dead men. 5 The angel answered the women, "Don't be afraid, for I know that you seek Jesus, who has been crucified. 6 He is not here, for he has risen, just like he said. Come, see the place where the Lord was lying. 7 Go quickly and tell his disciples, 'He has risen from the dead, and behold, he goes before you into Galilee; there you will see him.' Behold, I have told you."

Acts 1:1-3
The first book I wrote, Theophilus, concerned all that Jesus began both to do and to teach, 2 until the day in which he was received up, after he had given commandment through the Holy Spirit to the apostles whom he had chosen. 3 To these he also showed himself alive after he suffered, by many proofs, appearing to them over a period of forty days, and speaking about God's Kingdom.

Luke 24:50-53

50 He led them out as far as Bethany, and he lifted up his hands, and blessed them. 51 While he blessed them, he withdrew from them, and was carried up into heaven. 52 They worshiped him, and returned to Jerusalem with great joy, 53 and were continually in the temple, praising and blessing God. Amen.

Mark 16:19
So then the Lord, after he had spoken to them, was received up into heaven, and sat down at the right hand of God.

19 * * *

Acts 2:24
whom God raised up, having freed him from the agony of death, because it was not possible that he should be held by it.

1 Corinthians 15:54-57
54 But when this perishable body will have become imperishable, and this mortal will have put on immortality, then what is written will happen: "Death is swallowed up in victory." 55 "Death, where is your sting? Hades (or, Hell), where is your victory?" 56 The sting of death is sin, and the power of sin is the law. 57 But thanks be to God, who gives us the victory through our Lord Jesus Christ.

Hebrews 2:14
Since then the children have shared in flesh and blood, he also himself in the same way partook of the same, that through death he might bring to nothing him who had the power of death, that is, the devil,

20 * * *

Romans 3:21-26
21 But now apart from the law, a righteousness of God has been revealed, being testified by the law and the prophets; 22 even the righteousness of God through faith in Jesus Christ to all and on all those who believe. For there is no distinction, 23 for all have sinned, and fall short of the glory of God; 24 being justified freely by his grace through the redemption that is in Christ Jesus; 25 whom God sent to be an atoning sacrifice (or, a propitiation), through faith in his blood, for a demonstration of his

righteousness through the passing over of prior sins, in God's forbearance; 26 to demonstrate his righteousness at this present time; that he might himself be just, and the justifier of him who has faith in Jesus.

Romans 4:5-8
5 But to him who doesn't work, but believes in him who justifies the ungodly, his faith is accounted for righteousness. 6 Even as David also pronounces blessing on the man to whom God counts righteousness apart from works, 7 "Blessed are they whose iniquities are forgiven, whose sins are covered. 8 Blessed is the man whom the Lord will by no means charge with sin."

2 Timothy 1:10
but has now been revealed by the appearing of our Savior, Christ Jesus, who abolished death, and brought life and immortality to light through the Good News.

21 * * *
John 5:25-26
25 Most certainly I tell you, the hour comes, and now is, when the dead will hear the Son of God's voice; and those who hear will live. 26 For as the Father has life in himself, even so he gave to the Son also to have life in himself.

Romans 8:11
But if the Spirit of him who raised up Jesus from the dead dwells in you, he who raised up Christ Jesus from the dead will also give life to your mortal bodies through his Spirit who dwells in you.

22 * * *
1 Corinthians 15:35-49
35 But someone will say, "How are the dead raised?" and, "With what kind of body do they come?" 36 You foolish one, that which you yourself sow is not made alive unless it dies. 37 That which you sow, you don't sow the body that will be, but a bare grain, maybe of wheat, or of some other kind. 38 But God gives it a body even as it pleased him, and to each seed a body of its own. 39 All flesh is not the same flesh, but there is one flesh of men, another flesh of

animals, another of fish, and another of birds. 40 There are also celestial bodies and terrestrial bodies; but the glory of the celestial differs from that of the terrestrial. 41 There is one glory of the sun, another glory of the moon, and another glory of the stars; for one star differs from another star in glory. 42 So also is the resurrection of the dead. The body is sown perishable; it is raised imperishable. 43 It is sown in dishonor; it is raised in glory. It is sown in weakness; it is raised in power. 44 It is sown a natural body; it is raised a spiritual body. There is a natural body and there is also a spiritual body. 45 So also it is written, "The first man, Adam, became a living soul." The last Adam became a life-giving spirit. 46 However that which is spiritual isn't first, but that which is natural, then that which is spiritual. 47 The first man is of the earth, made of dust. The second man is the Lord from heaven. 48 As is the one made of dust, such are those who are also made of dust; and as is the heavenly, such are they also that are heavenly. 49 As we have borne the image of those made of dust, let's also bear the image of the heavenly.

Romans 8:22-23
22 For we know that the whole creation groans and travails in pain together until now. 23 Not only so, but ourselves also, who have the first fruits of the Spirit, even we ourselves groan within ourselves, waiting for adoption, the redemption of our body.

Chapter 8

THE ONLY SENSIBLE CHOICE

Now this point of *choice* is a vital issue to pause and reflect upon, because it boils down to an individual, personal decision. Everyone is ultimately responsible for himself and has no option to deflect that responsibility onto anyone else.[1]

So as an example, faithfully following the false teachings of any spiritual or religious leader or organization is not a legitimate excuse for not following the teachings of Jesus Himself. Just as ignorance of a speed limit does not excuse a driver from getting a speeding ticket, so it is also that ignorance of God's laws does not excuse anyone from the penalty associated with breaking them. It definitely is true that Jesus died for all of mankind, but that does not mean that everyone automatically gets to be with God when they die. Certainly, that is His desire, however He already knows that will not happen. Many people reject Him, His ways, His truth, His Son.[2]

Those who get to enjoy the privilege of eternal life are those who acknowledge that they are sinners, choose to turn away from sin,[3] believe in what Jesus did for them,[4] and acknowledge their faith for everlasting life in the finished work of Jesus Christ.[5] Failure to do so results in separation from God by confinement to eternal suffering in hell.[6] The Scriptures are very clear that hell is a real place which was originally intended for the fallen angels. Now, it is the final destination of anyone who remains rebellious to God, choosing to reject the gift of His Son.[7] There is no middle ground; there's either heaven or hell, and there is no option to earn one's way into heaven by doing good deeds; not before dying and certainly not after dying either.[8] The choice that must be made is to put one's faith in Jesus' sacrifice or not.[9] God does not send anyone to hell; rather, an individual chooses hell instead of doing things God's way.

The Gift of the Holy Spirit

Whoever makes that choice of putting their faith in Jesus is exceedingly blessed by being given the Holy Spirit.[10] At that moment of decision the spirit of the person is *regenerated* or *born again* by the Spirit of God.[11] This is a spiritual, but very real, gift from God. When this happens, the Holy Spirit, the third Person of God, actually lives within the person.[12] Such a spiritual transaction is difficult to comprehend with the natural mind to be sure. Still, most people will readily acknowledge that they have a human spirit which is distinct from their body, though they cannot see or understand its makeup. The Holy Spirit abides in the human body just as the human spirit does.

What was lost so long ago in the Garden of Eden has now, through the gift of Jesus, at least in some measure been restored. The barrier created by sin which previously separated mankind from God has been demolished. The born-again individual now has the privilege, the ability and the delight of drawing close to and getting to know the Creator of the universe. The primary way to deepen this relationship is to study the Holy Bible, which is the Word of God, with the Holy Spirit as one's primary teacher.[13] Anyone who does so, and is obedient to what is taught, is increasingly changed to be more like Jesus.[14] Consequently he is increasingly empowered to be more effective in making a positive difference in the world.

Guaranteed Eternal Life

The Holy Spirit is given as a down payment, guaranteeing one's eternal life.[15] This also comes with a conscious certainty of heart so that the individual knows, beyond a doubt, that he is safely in the hands of the living God.[16] Some will say that they "think" they are born again, or that the Holy Spirit is with them, but intellectual acceptance of a formal religious teaching falls far short of what God has provided. If an unquestionable certainty of heart is not present, then that person has serious reason to question his standing with God.

The Holy Spirit graciously provides a "knowing" that is independent of any intellectual reasoning.[17] When anyone has been granted eternal life by the grace of God, that individual is also given a heartfelt assurance, a supreme confidence, that his life has been secured. Such persons don't just "think" they are born again; they are "positive" that they are born again. Consequently, they know that if they were to die today, regardless of any past or present sins, they would still live forever with God, saved from the torment of hell. There are already a great many people worldwide who will readily attest to the fact that it is the Holy Spirit who gives that supernatural confidence. These are the people who make up the one true Church of Jesus Christ.

Chapter 8 References:

----

1 * * *

Romans 14:12
12 So then each one of us will give account of himself to God.

Matthew 12:36
36 I tell you that every idle word that men speak, they will give account of it in the day of judgment.

1 Peter 4:5
5 They will give account to him who is ready to judge the living and the dead.

2 * * *

Hebrews 4:13
13 There is no creature that is hidden from his sight, but all things are naked and laid open before the eyes of him to whom we must give an account.

Luke 16:15
15 He said to them, "You are those who justify yourselves in the sight of men, but God knows your hearts. For that which is exalted among men is an abomination in the sight of God.

Matthew 7:13-14
13 "Enter in by the narrow gate; for the gate is wide and the way is broad that leads to destruction, and there are many who enter in by it. 14 How the gate is narrow and the way is restricted that leads to life! There are who find it.

3 * * *

Psalm 130:1-4 (ESV)
1 Out of the depths I cry to you, O LORD! 2 O Lord, hear my voice! Let your ears be attentive to the voice of my pleas for mercy! 3 If you, O LORD, should mark iniquities, O Lord, who could stand? 4 But with you there is forgiveness, that you may be feared.

Romans 3:23

23 for all have sinned, and fall short of the glory of God;

4 * * *

Acts 4:12
12 There is salvation in no one else, for there is no other name under heaven that is given among men, by which we must be saved!"

John 3:16-17
16 For God so loved the world, that he gave his one and only Son, that whoever believes in him should not perish, but have eternal life. 17 For God didn't send his Son into the world to judge the world, but that the world should be saved through him.

John 20:31
31 but these are written, that you may believe that Jesus is the Christ, the Son of God, and that believing you may have life in his name.

Acts 10:43
43 All the prophets testify about him, that through his name everyone who believes in him will receive remission of sins."

5 * * *

Romans 10:8-10
8 But what does it say? "The word is near you, in your mouth, and in your heart;" that is, the word of faith which we preach: 9 that if you will confess with your mouth that Jesus is Lord, and believe in your heart that God raised him from the dead, you will be saved. 10 For with the heart, one believes resulting in righteousness; and with the mouth confession is made resulting in salvation.

Mark 1:15
15 and saying, "The time is fulfilled, and God's Kingdom is at hand! Repent, and believe in the Good News."

6 * * *

Matthew 5:29-30

[29] If your right eye causes you to stumble, pluck it out and throw it away from you. For it is more profitable for you that one of your members should perish than for your whole body to be cast into Gehenna. (or, Hell) [30] If your right hand causes you to stumble, cut it off, and throw it away from you. For it is more profitable for you that one of your members should perish, than for your whole body to be cast into Gehenna. (or, Hell)

Luke 12:5
[5] But I will warn you whom you should fear. Fear him who after he has killed, has power to cast into Gehenna. (or, Hell) Yes, I tell you, fear him.

2 Thessalonians 1:5-10
[5] This is an obvious sign of the righteous judgment of God, to the end that you may be counted worthy of God's Kingdom, for which you also suffer. [6] Since it is a righteous thing with God to repay affliction to those who afflict you, [7] and to give relief to you who are afflicted with us, when the Lord Jesus is revealed from heaven with his mighty angels in flaming fire, [8] punishing those who don't know God, and to those who don't obey the Good News of our Lord Jesus, [9] who will pay the penalty: eternal destruction from the face of the Lord and from the glory of his might, [10] when he comes in that day to be glorified in his saints and to be admired among all those who have believed, because our testimony to you was believed.

[7] * * *
Matthew 10:28
[28] Don't be afraid of those who kill the body, but are not able to kill the soul. Rather, fear him who is able to destroy both soul and body in Gehenna. (or, Hell)

Matthew 25:41
[41] Then he will say also to those on the left hand, 'Depart from me, you cursed, into the eternal fire which is prepared for the devil and his angels;

[8] * * *

Ephesians 2:8-9
[8] for by grace you have been saved through faith, and that not of yourselves; it is the gift of God, [9] not of works, that no one would boast.

Romans 3:26-28
[26] to demonstrate his righteousness at this present time; that he might himself be just, and the justifier of him who has faith in Jesus. [27] Where then is the boasting? It is excluded. By what kind of law? Of works? No, but by a law of faith. [28] We maintain therefore that a man is justified by faith apart from the works of the law.

Hebrews 9:27
[27] Inasmuch as it is appointed for men to die once, and after this, judgment,

Philippians 1:23
[23] But I am hard pressed between the two, having the desire to depart and be with Christ, which is far better.

[9] * * *

1 John 5:10-12
[10] He who believes in the Son of God has the testimony in himself. He who doesn't believe God has made him a liar, because he has not believed in the testimony that God has given concerning his Son. [11] The testimony is this, that God gave to us eternal life, and this life is in his Son. [12] He who has the Son has the life. He who doesn't have God's Son doesn't have the life.

John 11:25-26
[25] Jesus said to her, "I am the resurrection and the life. He who believes in me will still live, even if he dies. [26] Whoever lives and believes in me will never die. Do you believe this?"

[10] * * *

Mark 1:8
[8] I baptized you in water, but he will baptize you in the Holy Spirit."

_____

Romans 8:9

9 But you are not in the flesh but in the Spirit, if it is so that the Spirit of God dwells in you. But if any man doesn't have the Spirit of Christ, he is not his.

11 * * *

John 3:3-8

3 Jesus answered him, "Most certainly, I tell you, unless one is born anew, (The word translated "anew" here and in John 3:7 also means "again" and "from above".) he can't see God's Kingdom." 4 Nicodemus said to him, "How can a man be born when he is old? Can he enter a second time into his mother's womb, and be born?" 5 Jesus answered, "Most certainly I tell you, unless one is born of water and spirit, he can't enter into God's Kingdom. 6 That which is born of the flesh is flesh. That which is born of the Spirit is spirit. 7 Don't marvel that I said to you, 'You must be born anew.' 8 The wind (The same Greek word means wind, breath, and spirit.) blows where it wants to, and you hear its sound, but don't know where it comes from and where it is going. So is everyone who is born of the Spirit."

Acts 2:38

38 Peter said to them, "Repent, and be baptized, every one of you, in the name of Jesus Christ for the forgiveness of sins, and you will receive the gift of the Holy Spirit.

12 * * *

1 John 3:24

24 He who keeps his commandments remains in him, and he in him. By this we know that he remains in us, by the Spirit which he gave us.

1 John 4:12-16

12 No one has seen God at any time. If we love one another, God remains in us, and his love has been perfected in us. 13 By this we know that we remain in him and he in us, because he has given us of his Spirit. 14 We have seen and testify that the Father has sent the Son as the Savior of the world. 15 Whoever confesses that Jesus

is the Son of God, God remains in him, and he in God. [16] We know and have believed the love which God has for us. God is love, and he who remains in love remains in God, and God remains in him.

13 * * *
John 16:12-15
[12] "I still have many things to tell you, but you can't bear them now. [13] However when he, the Spirit of truth, has come, he will guide you into all truth, for he will not speak from himself; but whatever he hears, he will speak. He will declare to you things that are coming. [14] He will glorify me, for he will take from what is mine, and will declare it to you. [15] All things that the Father has are mine; therefore I said that he takes of mine and will declare it to you.

Hebrews 4:12
[12] For the word of God is living and active, and sharper than any two-edged sword, piercing even to the dividing of soul and spirit, of both joints and marrow, and is able to discern the thoughts and intentions of the heart.

14 * * *
Ephesians 5:25-27
[25] Husbands, love your wives, even as Christ also loved the assembly, and gave himself up for it; [26] that he might sanctify it, having cleansed it by the washing of water with the word, [27] that he might present the assembly to himself gloriously, not having spot or wrinkle or any such thing; but that it should be holy and without defect.

2 Corinthians 3:18
[18] But we all, with unveiled face seeing the glory of the Lord as in a mirror, are transformed into the same image from glory to glory, even as from the Lord, the Spirit.

2 Thessalonians 2:14
[14] to which he called you through our Good News, for the obtaining of the glory of our Lord Jesus Christ.

James 1:22-25

[22] But be doers of the word, and not only hearers, deluding your own selves. [23] For if anyone is a hearer of the word and not a doer, he is like a man looking at his natural face in a mirror; [24] for he sees himself, and goes away, and immediately forgets what kind of man he was. [25] But he who looks into the perfect law of freedom and continues, not being a hearer who forgets, but a doer of the work, this man will be blessed in what he does.

[15] * * *

2 Corinthians 5:5
[5] Now he who made us for this very thing is God, who also gave to us the down payment of the Spirit.

Ephesians 1:13-14
[13] In him you also, having heard the word of the truth, the Good News of your salvation—in whom, having also believed, you were sealed with the promised Holy Spirit, [14] who is a pledge of our inheritance, to the redemption of God's own possession, to the praise of his glory.

Ephesians 4:30
[30] Don't grieve the Holy Spirit of God, in whom you were sealed for the day of redemption.

[16] * * *

Hebrews 10:14-23
[14] For by one offering he has perfected forever those who are being sanctified. [15] The Holy Spirit also testifies to us, for after saying, [16] "This is the covenant that I will make with them: 'After those days,' says the Lord, 'I will put my laws on their heart, I will also write them on their mind;'" then he says, [17] "I will remember their sins and their iniquities no more." [18] Now where remission of these is, there is no more offering for sin. [19] Having therefore, brothers, boldness to enter into the holy place by the blood of Jesus, [20] by the way which he dedicated for us, a new and living way, through the veil, that is to say, his flesh, [21] and having a great priest over God's house, [22] let's draw near with a true heart in fullness of faith, having our hearts sprinkled from an evil conscience, and having

our body washed with pure water, 23 let's hold fast the confession of our hope without wavering; for he who promised is faithful.

Colossians 2:2
2 that their hearts may be comforted, they being knit together in love, and gaining all riches of the full assurance of understanding, that they may know the mystery of God, both of the Father and of Christ,

17 * * *
Romans 8:14-17
14 For as many as are led by the Spirit of God, these are children of God. 15 For you didn't receive the spirit of bondage again to fear, but you received the Spirit of adoption, by whom we cry, "Abba! Father!" (Abba is an Aramaic word for "Father" or "Daddy", which can be used affectionately and respectfully in prayer to our Father in heaven.) 16 The Spirit himself testifies with our spirit that we are children of God; 17 and if children, then heirs: heirs of God and joint heirs with Christ, if indeed we suffer with him, that we may also be glorified with him.

1 John 5:13
13 These things I have written to you who believe in the name of the Son of God, that you may know that you have eternal life, and that you may continue to believe in the name of the Son of God.

Chapter 9

ONE SPIRITUAL BODY

Previous chapters described how mankind has repeatedly failed at rising up to fulfill God's purposes for him on Earth. His chosen representatives started out with a right heart and doing things His way but ended up off course. Both ancient and current history show that if man rebels against the way of God, his best efforts ultimately will result in failure, even if he realizes some success in the natural along the way. The time in which we live, which is known as the Church age, so far has demonstrated much of the same behavior.

The Church is Started

The Son of God, Jesus Christ, gave up the riches and glory of heaven to come to Earth to save mankind.[1] He bore rejection, insults, torture and death on a cross to pay the price for our sin.[2] However before He died Jesus spent about three years giving twelve men concentrated teaching and example of God's way of living.[3] These were the initial and primary ones designated to spread His teaching, but many other disciples were added to them at the time and ever since.[4] After Jesus ascended back into heaven, God then sent the Holy Spirit to the Earth to fill and empower each of the disciples of Jesus.[5] This was the official start of the "Church". The word "church" means a called-out assembly. So, similar to how the Israelite nation was formed and spiritually separated from the world to represent God, so too is the Church called out of living sinful lives to give glory to God.[6]

Servants of God

The Church is God's divinely created and chosen representative on Earth today.[7] Just as He did in past generations, God desires to accomplish His present-day objectives through the lives of men, women and children who desire to willingly serve Him. God created Adam and Eve for a purpose; He saved Noah and family for a purpose; He brought forth Israel for a purpose; and He created the Church for a purpose. His agenda now is to work through the Church to manifest His very nature to mankind and to evil spiritual beings as well.[8] In this way the works of the devil will be increasingly exposed and many people will be reconciled to God, drawn to following the way of Jesus.

God has made it clear in His Holy Scriptures however, that many people will not choose His way.[9] For those who do, the privilege and honor comes with divine expectation and responsibility, at a cost. That cost is one that is paid by way of separation from the ways of the world to the ways of God.[10] No member of the Church is forced by God to make any greater commitment to His purposes than he personally is willing to. Still, be aware that the degree of sacrificial commitment of every individual will be met with comparable rewards in heaven.[11] Also, be aware that every believer in Jesus will find no greater joy on Earth than in accomplishing those things which the Lord has appointed for him to do.[12]

Members of the Church

It can easily and quickly be seen from past as well as recent history that the Church has failed in many ways, just like its predecessors did. In teachings and in practice, many things which are contrary to God's way have infiltrated and polluted what Jesus started. Still, throughout the world today, there are a core group of Church members who are firmly focused on serving the Lord in His way and for His honor. That's not to suggest that any one of these people is perfect and doesn't make mistakes. Nor does it say that any individual, local church body, national or international organization, perfectly understands and represents the Lord in all His ways. What it does say however is that there are many people who are primarily committed to serving the Lord, not to serving a religion, institution or individual human being. At the very core of their being, what they want most in life is to be one in heart and mind and will with God. It has been that way since the creation of the Church, and it will be that way until this age comes to its end.

The True Church of God is Not an Earthly Organization

The Church is also known as "the Body of Christ", with Jesus as its Head, so together with Him the Church accomplishes His goals on Earth.[13] God's grace makes it all possible.[14] From when the Church was started, and continuing through today, it consists of all those who choose to put their faith for eternal life in the completed work of Jesus.[15] Association with any formal religion, past, present or future has no bearing on any individual's membership in the Church.

The true and only Church of God is not defined or identified by having a personal connection with an earthly organization. Rather, it is defined by having a direct and personal relationship with the God of the universe, through Jesus, being led by the Spirit of God to do things His way.[16] All those who commit their hearts to the way of Jesus Christ become brothers and sisters in the family of God.[17] The Church transcends tribes, nations, languages, organized religion, and geographical boundaries.[18] It is not a building and it is not a man-made organization of any type, but a spiritual body; a people called out and fashioned by the hand of God Himself. That said, it is still important for the Church to gather together for many reasons, especially to worship Him and to seek and understand the truth of God.[19]

The Church is Empowered to Overcome

In addition to paying the price for our sins, God also made it possible for everyone to overcome the temptations to sin.[20] Jesus Himself made the way by overcoming every temptation that could come upon mankind, though in His case He did it perfectly and we do not.[21] He has given man the opportunity to become in essence a new creation; taught, emboldened and empowered by the Holy Spirit to change from our sinful ways.[22] When anyone is born again and is challenged with any temptation to sin, the Holy Spirit brings the issue into focus as something which needs to be addressed and also gives us the ability to turn away from it.[23] In this ever-deepening, two-way, loving relationship, the Holy Spirit works at changing our heart to be in alignment with His.[24] With every change towards becoming more like Jesus, the Body of Christ increasingly reflects His life in the world.[25] It is a powerful, amazing, spiritual transformation that is initiated by God, touches the life of one person, who then continues to grow and touches the lives of many other people with the goodness of God.[26]

In the history of man there have been many times, and certainly the time in which we live, when God has postponed bringing the full force of His judgment to bear. With great patience and enormous mercy and in the depth of His love, He gives mankind ample opportunity to turn from his evil ways. Still, there is no reason to think that He will go on indefinitely being so gracious. On the contrary, it appears in His Scriptures that the Church embodies His last human entity to affect His purposes on Earth prior to His return. Once those things are completed, He will come to bring judgment, as the insights in the next chapter will reveal.

Chapter 9 References:

[1] * * *

John 1:1-5
In the beginning was the Word, and the Word was with God, and the Word was God. [2] The same was in the beginning with God. [3] All things were made through him. Without him, nothing was made that has been made. [4] In him was life, and the life was the light of men. [5] The light shines in the darkness, and the darkness hasn't overcome it.

John 8:58
[58] Jesus said to them, "Most certainly, I tell you, before Abraham came into existence, I AM."

John 17:5
[5] Now, Father, glorify me with your own self with the glory which I had with you before the world existed.

[2] * * *
Isaiah 53:3

---

3 He was despised and rejected by men, a man of suffering and acquainted with disease. He was despised as one from whom men hide their face; and we didn't respect him.

Matthew 20:17-19
17 As Jesus was going up to Jerusalem, he took the twelve disciples aside, and on the way he said to them, 18 "Behold, we are going up to Jerusalem, and the Son of Man will be delivered to the chief priests and scribes, and they will condemn him to death, 19 and will hand him over to the Gentiles to mock, to scourge, and to crucify; and the third day he will be raised up."

Matthew 26:65-68
65 Then the high priest tore his clothing, saying, "He has spoken blasphemy! Why do we need any more witnesses? Behold, now you have heard his blasphemy. 66 What do you think?" They answered, "He is worthy of death!" 67 Then they spat in his face and beat him with their fists, and some slapped him, 68 saying, "Prophesy to us, you Christ! Who hit you?"

Mark 15:16-20
16 And the soldiers led him away inside the palace (that is, the governor's headquarters), and they called together the whole battalion. 17 And they clothed him in a purple cloak, and twisting together a crown of thorns, they put it on him. 18 And they began to salute him, "Hail, King of the Jews!" 19 And they were striking his head with a reed and spitting on him and kneeling down in homage to him. 20 And when they had mocked him, they stripped him of the purple cloak and put his own clothes on him. And they led him out to crucify him.

3 * * *
John 17:6-8
6 I revealed your name to the people whom you have given me out of the world. They were yours, and you have given them to me. They have kept your word. 7 Now they have known that all things whatever you have given me are from you, 8 for the words which you have given me I have given to them, and they received them,

and knew for sure that I came from you. They have believed that you sent me.

Luke 6:12-13
¹² In these days, he went out to the mountain to pray, and he continued all night in prayer to God. ¹³ When it was day, he called his disciples, and from them he chose twelve, whom he also named apostles:

4 * * *
Acts 1:15
¹⁵ In these days, Peter stood up in the middle of the disciples (and the number of names was about one hundred twenty), and said,

Acts 9:31
³¹ So the assemblies throughout all Judea, Galilee, and Samaria had peace, and were built up. They were multiplied, walking in the fear of the Lord and in the comfort of the Holy Spirit.

5 * * *
Acts 1:4-5
⁴ Being assembled together with them, he commanded them, "Don't depart from Jerusalem, but wait for the promise of the Father, which you heard from me. ⁵ For John indeed baptized in water, but you will be baptized in the Holy Spirit not many days from now."

Acts 2:1-4
Now when the day of Pentecost had come, they were all with one accord in one place. ² Suddenly there came from the sky a sound like the rushing of a mighty wind, and it filled all the house where they were sitting. ³ Tongues like fire appeared and were distributed to them, and one sat on each of them. ⁴ They were all filled with the Holy Spirit, and began to speak with other languages, as the Spirit gave them the ability to speak.

6 * * *
Ephesians 2:19-22

¹⁹ So then you are no longer strangers and foreigners, but you are fellow citizens with the saints and of the household of God, ²⁰ being built on the foundation of the apostles and prophets, Christ Jesus himself being the chief cornerstone; ²¹ in whom the whole building, fitted together, grows into a holy temple in the Lord; ²² in whom you also are built together for a habitation of God in the Spirit.

Ephesians 4:17-24
¹⁷ This I say therefore, and testify in the Lord, that you no longer walk as the rest of the Gentiles also walk, in the futility of their mind, ¹⁸ being darkened in their understanding, alienated from the life of God because of the ignorance that is in them, because of the hardening of their hearts. ¹⁹ They, having become callous, gave themselves up to lust, to work all uncleanness with greediness. ²⁰ But you didn't learn Christ that way, ²¹ if indeed you heard him, and were taught in him, even as truth is in Jesus: ²² that you put away, as concerning your former way of life, the old man that grows corrupt after the lusts of deceit, ²³ and that you be renewed in the spirit of your mind, ²⁴ and put on the new man, who in the likeness of God has been created in righteousness and holiness of truth.

Philippians 2:14-16
¹⁴ Do all things without complaining and arguing, ¹⁵ that you may become blameless and harmless, children of God without defect in the middle of a crooked and perverse generation, among whom you are seen as lights in the world, ¹⁶ holding up the word of life, that I may have something to boast in the day of Christ, that I didn't run in vain nor labor in vain.

7 * * *

Ephesians 1:3-6
3 Blessed be the God and Father of our Lord Jesus Christ, who has blessed us with every spiritual blessing in the heavenly places in Christ, 4 even as he chose us in him before the foundation of the world, that we would be holy and without defect before him in love, 5 having predestined us for adoption as children through Jesus Christ to himself, according to the good pleasure of his

desire, [6] to the praise of the glory of his grace, by which he freely gave us favor in the Beloved,

1 Peter 2:9-12
[9] But you are a chosen race, a royal priesthood, a holy nation, a people for God's own possession, that you may proclaim the excellence of him who called you out of darkness into his marvelous light. [10] In the past, you were not a people, but now are God's people, who had not obtained mercy, but now have obtained mercy. [11] Beloved, I beg you as foreigners and pilgrims, to abstain from fleshly lusts, which war against the soul; [12] having good behavior among the nations, so in that of which they speak against you as evildoers, they may by your good works, which they see, glorify God in the day of visitation.

[8] * * *

2 Corinthians 5:18-21
[18] But all things are of God, who reconciled us to himself through Jesus Christ, and gave to us the ministry of reconciliation; [19] namely, that God was in Christ reconciling the world to himself, not reckoning to them their trespasses, and having committed to us the word of reconciliation. [20] We are therefore ambassadors on behalf of Christ, as though God were entreating by us: we beg you on behalf of Christ, be reconciled to God. [21] For him who knew no sin he made to be sin on our behalf; so that in him we might become the righteousness of God.

Ephesians 3:8-10
[8] To me, the very least of all saints, was this grace given, to preach to the Gentiles the unsearchable riches of Christ, [9] and to make all men see what is the administration of the mystery which for ages has been hidden in God, who created all things through Jesus Christ, [10] to the intent that now through the assembly the manifold wisdom of God might be made known to the principalities and the powers in the heavenly places,

[9] * * *
Matthew 13:47-50

47 "Again, the Kingdom of Heaven is like a dragnet that was cast into the sea and gathered some fish of every kind, 48 which, when it was filled, fishermen drew up on the beach. They sat down and gathered the good into containers, but the bad they threw away. 49 So will it be in the end of the world. (or, end of the age) The angels will come and separate the wicked from among the righteous, 50 and will cast them into the furnace of fire. There will be weeping and gnashing of teeth."

Matthew 22:1-14

Jesus answered and spoke to them again in parables, saying, 2 "The Kingdom of Heaven is like a certain king, who made a wedding feast for his son, 3 and sent out his servants to call those who were invited to the wedding feast, but they would not come. 4 Again he sent out other servants, saying, 'Tell those who are invited, "Behold, I have prepared my dinner. My cattle and my fatlings are killed, and all things are ready. Come to the wedding feast!"' 5 But they made light of it, and went their ways, one to his own farm, another to his merchandise; 6 and the rest grabbed his servants, treated them shamefully, and killed them. 7 When the king heard that, he was angry, and sent his armies, destroyed those murderers, and burned their city. 8 "Then he said to his servants, 'The wedding is ready, but those who were invited weren't worthy. 9 Go therefore to the intersections of the highways, and as many as you may find, invite to the wedding feast.' 10 Those servants went out into the highways and gathered together as many as they found, both bad and good. The wedding was filled with guests. 11 "But when the king came in to see the guests, he saw there a man who didn't have on wedding clothing, 12 and he said to him, 'Friend, how did you come in here not wearing wedding clothing?' He was speechless. 13 Then the king said to the servants, 'Bind him hand and foot, take him away, and throw him into the outer darkness. That is where the weeping and grinding of teeth will be.' 14 For many are called, but few chosen."

10 * * *

Matthew 10:21-25

21 "Brother will deliver up brother to death, and the father his child. Children will rise up against parents and cause them to be put to death. 22 You will be hated by all men for my name's sake, but he who endures to the end will be saved. 23 But when they persecute you in this city, flee into the next, for most certainly I tell you, you will not have gone through the cities of Israel until the Son of Man has come. 24 "A disciple is not above his teacher, nor a servant above his lord. 25 It is enough for the disciple that he be like his teacher, and the servant like his lord. If they have called the master of the house Beelzebul (literally, Lord of the Flies, or the devil), how much more those of his household!

John 15:18-21
18 If the world hates you, you know that it has hated me before it hated you. 19 If you were of the world, the world would love its own. But because you are not of the world, since I chose you out of the world, therefore the world hates you. 20 Remember the word that I said to you: 'A servant is not greater than his lord.' If they persecuted me, they will also persecute you. If they kept my word, they will also keep yours. 21 But they will do all these things to you for my name's sake, because they don't know him who sent me.

John 17:14-20
14 I have given them your word. The world hated them, because they are not of the world, even as I am not of the world. 15 I pray not that you would take them from the world, but that you would keep them from the evil one. 16 They are not of the world even as I am not of the world. 17 Sanctify them in your truth. Your word is truth. 18 As you sent me into the world, even so I have sent them into the world. 19 For their sakes I sanctify myself, that they themselves also may be sanctified in truth. 20 Not for these only do I pray, but for those also who will believe in me through their word,

11 * * *

Matthew 16:27
27 For the Son of Man will come in the glory of his Father with his angels, and then he will render to everyone according to his deeds.

Luke 6:22-23
²² Blessed are you when men hate you, and when they exclude and mock you, and throw out your name as evil, for the Son of Man's sake. ²³ Rejoice in that day, and leap for joy, for behold, your reward is great in heaven, for their fathers did the same thing to the prophets.

1 Corinthians 3:11-15
¹¹ For no one can lay any other foundation than that which has been laid, which is Jesus Christ. ¹² But if anyone builds on the foundation with gold, silver, costly stones, wood, hay, or stubble, ¹³ each man's work will be revealed. For the Day will declare it, because it is revealed in fire; and the fire itself will test what sort of work each man's work is. ¹⁴ If any man's work remains which he built on it, he will receive a reward. ¹⁵ If any man's work is burned, he will suffer loss, but he himself will be saved, but as through fire.

12 * * *

Ephesians 2:10
¹⁰ For we are his workmanship, created in Christ Jesus for good works, which God prepared before that we would walk in them.

Acts 13:50-52
⁵⁰ But the Jews stirred up the devout and prominent women and the chief men of the city, and stirred up a persecution against Paul and Barnabas, and threw them out of their borders. ⁵¹ But they shook off the dust of their feet against them, and came to Iconium. ⁵² The disciples were filled with joy and with the Holy Spirit.

13 * * *

1 Corinthians 12:12-14
¹² For as the body is one, and has many members, and all the members of the body, being many, are one body; so also is Christ. ¹³ For in one Spirit we were all baptized into one body, whether Jews or Greeks, whether bond or free; and were all given to drink into one Spirit. ¹⁴ For the body is not one member, but many.

Ephesians 1:22-23
22 He put all things in subjection under his feet, and gave him to be head over all things for the assembly, 23 which is his body, the fullness of him who fills all in all.

Ephesians 5:28-30
28 Even so husbands also ought to love their own wives as their own bodies. He who loves his own wife loves himself. 29 For no man ever hated his own flesh; but nourishes and cherishes it, even as the Lord also does the assembly; 30 because we are members of his body, of his flesh and bones.

Colossians 1:24
24 Now I rejoice in my sufferings for your sake, and fill up on my part that which is lacking of the afflictions of Christ in my flesh for his body's sake, which is the assembly,

14 * * *

John 1:17
17 For the law was given through Moses. Grace and truth were realized through Jesus Christ.

Acts 4:33
33 With great power, the apostles gave their testimony of the resurrection of the Lord Jesus. Great grace was on them all.

Acts 11:21-24
21 The hand of the Lord was with them, and a great number believed and turned to the Lord. 22 The report concerning them came to the ears of the assembly which was in Jerusalem. They sent out Barnabas to go as far as Antioch, 23 who, when he had come, and had seen the grace of God, was glad. He exhorted them all, that with purpose of heart they should remain near to the Lord. 24 For he was a good man, and full of the Holy Spirit and of faith, and many people were added to the Lord.

15 * * *

Ephesians 4:1-6

I therefore, the prisoner in the Lord, beg you to walk worthily of the calling with which you were called, 2 with all lowliness and humility, with patience, bearing with one another in love, 3 being eager to keep the unity of the Spirit in the bond of peace. 4 There is one body and one Spirit, even as you also were called in one hope of your calling, 5 one Lord, one faith, one baptism, 6 one God and Father of all, who is over all and through all, and in us all.

16 * * *
John 1:12-13
12 But as many as received him, to them he gave the right to become God's children, to those who believe in his name: 13 who were born not of blood, nor of the will of the flesh, nor of the will of man, but of God.

Romans 8:5
5 For those who live according to the flesh set their minds on the things of the flesh, but those who live according to the Spirit, the things of the Spirit.

Romans 8:14
14 For as many as are led by the Spirit of God, these are children of God.

Galatians 3:26
26 For you are all children of God, through faith in Christ Jesus.

17 * * *
Matthew 12:46-50
46 While he was yet speaking to the multitudes, behold, his mother and his brothers stood outside, seeking to speak to him. 47 One said to him, "Behold, your mother and your brothers stand outside, seeking to speak to you." 48 But he answered him who spoke to him, "Who is my mother? Who are my brothers?" 49 He stretched out his hand toward his disciples, and said, "Behold, my mother and my brothers! 50 For whoever does the will of my Father who is in heaven, he is my brother, and sister, and mother."

1 John 1:5-7

5 This is the message which we have heard from him and announce to you, that God is light, and in him is no darkness at all. 6 If we say that we have fellowship with him and walk in the darkness, we lie, and don't tell the truth. 7 But if we walk in the light, as he is in the light, we have fellowship with one another, and the blood of Jesus Christ, his Son, cleanses us from all sin.

18 * * *

1 Corinthians 1:2
2 to the assembly of God which is at Corinth—those who are sanctified in Christ Jesus, called saints, with all who call on the name of our Lord Jesus Christ in every place, both theirs and ours:

19 * * *

Colossians 3:16
16 Let the word of Christ dwell in you richly; in all wisdom teaching and admonishing one another with psalms, hymns, and spiritual songs, singing with grace in your heart to the Lord.

Ephesians 4:11-16
11 He gave some to be apostles; and some, prophets; and some, evangelists; and some, shepherds (or, pastors) and teachers; 12 for the perfecting of the saints, to the work of serving, to the building up of the body of Christ, 13 until we all attain to the unity of the faith and of the knowledge of the Son of God, to a full grown man, to the measure of the stature of the fullness of Christ, 14 that we may no longer be children, tossed back and forth and carried about with every wind of doctrine, by the trickery of men, in craftiness, after the wiles of error; 15 but speaking truth in love, we may grow up in all things into him who is the head, Christ, 16 from whom all the body, being fitted and knit together through that which every joint supplies, according to the working in measure of each individual part, makes the body increase to the building up of itself in love.

Hebrews 10:24-25
24 Let's consider how to provoke one another to love and good works, 25 not forsaking our own assembling together, as the

custom of some is, but exhorting one another, and so much the more as you see the Day approaching.

20 * * *

1 Corinthians 10:13
13 No temptation has taken you except what is common to man. God is faithful, who will not allow you to be tempted above what you are able, but will with the temptation also make the way of escape, that you may be able to endure it.

2 Peter 2:9
9 the Lord knows how to deliver the godly out of temptation and to keep the unrighteous under punishment for the day of judgment,

21 * * *

John 16:33
33 I have told you these things, that in me you may have peace. In the world you have trouble; but cheer up! I have overcome the world."

Hebrews 2:18
18 For in that he himself has suffered being tempted, he is able to help those who are tempted.

Hebrews 4:14-16
14 Having then a great high priest who has passed through the heavens, Jesus, the Son of God, let's hold tightly to our confession. 15 For we don't have a high priest who can't be touched with the feeling of our infirmities, but one who has been in all points tempted like we are, yet without sin. 16 Let's therefore draw near with boldness to the throne of grace, that we may receive mercy and may find grace for help in time of need.

22 * * *

2 Corinthians 5:17
17 Therefore if anyone is in Christ, he is a new creation. The old things have passed away. Behold, all things have become new.

John 16:12-15

12 "I still have many things to tell you, but you can't bear them now. 13 However when he, the Spirit of truth, has come, he will guide you into all truth, for he will not speak from himself; but whatever he hears, he will speak. He will declare to you things that are coming. 14 He will glorify me, for he will take from what is mine, and will declare it to you. 15 All things that the Father has are mine; therefore I said that he takes of mine and will declare it to you.

Acts 1:8
8 But you will receive power when the Holy Spirit has come upon you. You will be witnesses to me in Jerusalem, in all Judea and Samaria, and to the uttermost parts of the earth."

23 * * *
John 15:26
26 "When the Counselor (Greek Parakletos: Counselor, Helper, Advocate, Intercessor, and Comforter.) has come, whom I will send to you from the Father, the Spirit of truth, who proceeds from the Father, he will testify about me.

1 John 5:4
4 For whatever is born of God overcomes the world. This is the victory that has overcome the world: your faith.

24 * * *
John 14:26
26 But the Counselor, the Holy Spirit, whom the Father will send in my name, will teach you all things, and will remind you of all that I said to you.

1 Corinthians 2:10-13
10 But to us, God revealed them through the Spirit. For the Spirit searches all things, yes, the deep things of God. 11 For who among men knows the things of a man, except the spirit of the man, which is in him? Even so, no one knows the things of God, except God's Spirit. 12 But we received not the spirit of the world, but the Spirit which is from God, that we might know the things that were freely given to us by God. 13 We also speak these things, not in words

which man's wisdom teaches, but which the Holy Spirit teaches, comparing spiritual things with spiritual things.
25 * * *

1 Corinthians 6:19-20
Or don't you know that your body is a temple of the Holy Spirit who is in you, whom you have from God? You are not your own, 20 for you were bought with a price. Therefore glorify God in your body and in your spirit, which are God's.

Philippians 1:20
20 according to my earnest expectation and hope, that I will in no way be disappointed, but with all boldness, as always, now also Christ will be magnified in my body, whether by life or by death.

26 * * *

Matthew 5:14-16
14 You are the light of the world. A city located on a hill can't be hidden. 15 Neither do you light a lamp and put it under a measuring basket, but on a stand; and it shines to all who are in the house. 16 Even so, let your light shine before men, that they may see your good works and glorify your Father who is in heaven.

Matthew 28:18-20
18 Jesus came to them and spoke to them, saying, "All authority has been given to me in heaven and on earth. 19 Go and make disciples of all nations, baptizing them in the name of the Father and of the Son and of the Holy Spirit, 20 teaching them to observe all things that I commanded you. Behold, I am with you always, even to the end of the age." Amen.

Mark 16:15-18
15 He said to them, "Go into all the world, and preach the Good News to the whole creation. 16 He who believes and is baptized will be saved; but he who disbelieves will be condemned. 17 These signs will accompany those who believe: in my name they will cast out demons; they will speak with new languages; 18 they will take up serpents; and if they drink any deadly thing, it will in no way hurt them; they will lay hands on the sick, and they will recover."

Chapter 10

SPIRITUAL AND NATURAL MERGER

E ven though God has provided many details about what we can expect to see transpire in the future, putting those details together in a definitive way to paint a complete picture is challenging. On this point it must be noted that multiple narratives exist regarding the accurate interpretation of those details. What actual events may take place, their timing and sequence, and even specific nations and people involved are some examples of subjects still being discussed and debated.

The overview of future events contained in this chapter is not intended to be perceived as conclusive or dogmatic. Rather, it should simply be considered as a good possibility in the light of specific supporting Scriptures. The primary intention here is to shed some light on the fact that God has documented for us, in His Holy Bible, that He has very specific plans He intends to carry out to completion. All should simply continue to investigate these things, as God Himself expects us to.

An Incomplete Picture, but Not to be Ignored

A key point here is that regardless of our incomplete knowledge of the details or our limited understanding of them, it is foolish to completely disregard the information that is available. Anyone who blindly assumes that life will go on as we know it indefinitely, will leave himself on the path to eternal destruction. While this topic is not as clear cut as the previous ones, it's important to look at for several reasons. First, it's important to know that God does in fact have an agenda for the future of the world and all its people. Second, an increasing awareness of the details available will help to shape one's perspective and choices in life. Third, knowing and getting in sync with God's agenda will be a blessing for each individual, which will in turn enable each person to be a blessing to family and to others.

Do We Dare Try to Investigate the Future?

The idea of peering into God's long-term plans may seem brash and bold to some, yet He has clearly opened the door for anyone motivated to study His agenda. That being the case, it seems prudent that we should at least attempt to understand what He has provided, since this information is there for our benefit.[1] The Bible book of Revelation is a major resource detailing these future events, and the Lord promises a blessing to those who read and hear and stay true to what is written.[2] This is the only book in the bible to come with such a specific blessing, in which the Lord stresses the importance of looking beyond the immediate cares of life. The more we come to understand, the better able we are to make wise choices; and the more we examine what He has said He will do, the greater we will know Him as well. The Scriptures clearly show that the cycle of generations we are familiar with will definitely not go on forever.[3] In fact, when

Jesus came to Earth to live life as a man about 2000 years ago, that marked the beginning of the end of this age in God's eyes.[4] That alone should cause every one of us to stop and soberly evaluate our standing with Him.

History Reveals God's Way

The cycle of generations characterized by birth, life and death, seems like it will go on indefinitely, but that is not the case. The historical events noted earlier clearly show that while God is patient, merciful and loving, He is also a fair and just judge who hates and punishes sin. The devastation of virtually an entire civilization should make that point clear. The extremely well-documented history of the nation of Israel over many generations should firmly and finally settle the point that God does what He says He will do. With a great many past situations God specified ahead of time what He would do, and those events did in fact come to pass. Since He has also spoken of what He will do in the future, we can be assured that He will likewise bring these things to pass as well. God is not a liar. While no one knows the amount of time remaining before the last of the last days, the time is short.[5] While He may take what seems to the typical human being to be a very long time[6], the day inevitably arrives when the Lord steps in to take issue with those who are rebellious to Him, whether it is an individual, a nation or the entire world.

The Final Seven Years

Once the Gospel (which means "Good News") of Jesus Christ has been proclaimed throughout the nations, God will bring this present Church age to an end.[7] The timing of this will be simple for God, because He already knows those who will ultimately and finally reject Him; just as He also

---

knows all those who will accept Him.[8] The timing is not so clear for us to determine, however the Bible does identify a seven-year period which will be the final years of mankind as we know it.

This period will be tumultuous. Though it may begin with a temporary illusion of peace, it will be filled with wars, famine, unusual and catastrophic disasters, and death.[9] It primarily will be led by a powerful and brilliant leader known as the final anti-Christ, who will head up a world-wide government.[10] That government will be promoted and bolstered temporarily by a world-wide, but false, religion headed up by the person known as the false prophet.[11] Both of these people are agents of Satan.[12] Halfway into that seven year period the anti-Christ sets himself up as God, in the very temple of God in Jerusalem.[13] This initiates disasters of increasing intensity during the last three and a half years which is known as the Great Tribulation.[14] In that time even the world religion is torn down by the government.[15]

At some point, probably not long before the seven-year period begins, God will remove the true Church from the Earth, whether alive or already dead, taking them to be with Him in heaven.[16] Those still resisting God's way will remain on Earth, through the worst of God's judgments, until Jesus returns. Some people will have a change of heart in the midst of the disasters and yield to God's way, but many others will not and will therefore pay an eternal price for their foolishness.[17] While no one can say precisely when Jesus will return, God has indicated that the last seven year period will begin when the final antichrist confirms a covenant with Israel.[18] That covenant of peace will only last three and a half years however, following which the nation of Israel will be subjected to great oppression.

King Jesus Returns

At the end of the seven years Jesus will return to Earth.[19] When He first came as an infant born in Bethlehem, His purpose was to restore mankind's relationship with God.[20] When He returns at the end of the age however, His purpose will be to judge all those on Earth who refuse to accept His Way.[21] That point in mankind's history is often referred to as *The Day of the Lord*, and at that time also, the Israelite people will again return to the forefront of God's plans.[22] Although the greater percentage of them will die in the catastrophes that will take place, there will be a remnant that will survive and that will finally recognize and accept Jesus as their long-expected Messiah and Savior.[23]

Jesus Christ will come with His resurrected Church and His holy angels at the end of the seven years.[24] He will defeat the combined armies of nations, along with the spiritual forces of evil opposed to Him in the battle of Armageddon, and lock up Satan for a time.[25] The Lord will gather to Himself all those who have put their trust in Him, and will then set up an Earthly world-wide kingdom over which He will rule with righteousness and justice for a thousand years.[26] At the end of that time there will be a final battle with evil forces. The Lord will deal decisively with this rebellion and put a final end to Satan's efforts by casting him into hell forever.[27] At that time also, there will be a final judgment for all those throughout the history of man who refused to accept God's rule and His way. They will be eternally separated from Him, suffering in torment in hell.[28] God will remake the heavens and the Earth, and those who have accepted Him will live with Him for eternity, in a state of no sin or pain or suffering.[29] That is Good News indeed!

Chapter 10 References:

1 * * *

1 Corinthians 10:11
[11] Now all these things happened to them by way of example, and they were written for our admonition, on whom the ends of the ages have come.

2 Timothy 3:16
[16] Every Scripture is God-breathed and (or, Every writing inspired by God is) profitable for teaching, for reproof, for correction, and for instruction in righteousness,

2 * * *

Revelation 1:3
[3] Blessed is he who reads and those who hear the words of the prophecy, and keep the things that are written in it, for the time is at hand.

Revelation 22:7
[7] "Behold, I come quickly. Blessed is he who keeps the words of the prophecy of this book."

3 * * *

1 Peter 4:7
[7] But the end of all things is near. Therefore be of sound mind, self-controlled, and sober in prayer.

Romans 13:11-12
[11] Do this, knowing the time, that it is already time for you to awaken out of sleep, for salvation is now nearer to us than when we first believed. [12] The night is far gone, and the day is near. Let's therefore throw off the deeds of darkness, and let's put on the armor of light.

James 5:8

---

[8] You also be patient. Establish your hearts, for the coming of the Lord is at hand.

1 John 2:18
[18] Little children, these are the end times, and as you heard that the Antichrist is coming, even now many antichrists have arisen. By this we know that it is the final hour.

4 * * *
Hebrews 1:1-3
God, having in the past spoken to the fathers through the prophets at many times and in various ways, [2] has at the end of these days spoken to us by his Son, whom he appointed heir of all things, through whom also he made the worlds. [3] His Son is the radiance of his glory, the very image of his substance, and upholding all things by the word of his power, who, when he had by himself purified us of our sins, sat down on the right hand of the Majesty on high,

Hebrews 9:26
[26] or else he must have suffered often since the foundation of the world. But now once at the end of the ages, he has been revealed to put away sin by the sacrifice of himself.

1 Peter 1:20
[20] who was foreknown indeed before the foundation of the world, but was revealed in this last age for your sake,

5 * * *
Matthew 24:36-39
[36] "But no one knows of that day and hour, not even the angels of heaven, but my Father only. [37] As the days of Noah were, so will the coming of the Son of Man be. [38] For as in the days which were before the flood they were eating and drinking, marrying and giving in marriage, until the day that Noah entered into the ship, [39] and they didn't know until the flood came and took them all away, so will the coming of the Son of Man be.

Luke 12:40

---

[40] Therefore be ready also, for the Son of Man is coming in an hour that you don't expect him."

1 Corinthians 7:29-31

[29] But I say this, brothers: the time is short, that from now on, both those who have wives may be as though they had none; [30] and those who weep, as though they didn't weep; and those who rejoice, as though they didn't rejoice; and those who buy, as though they didn't possess; [31] and those who use the world, as not using it to the fullest. For the mode of this world passes away.

6 * * *

Romans 2:4

[4] Or do you despise the riches of his goodness, forbearance, and patience, not knowing that the goodness of God leads you to repentance?

2 Peter 3:8-9

[8] But don't forget this one thing, beloved, that one day is with the Lord as a thousand years, and a thousand years as one day. [9] The Lord is not slow concerning his promise, as some count slowness; but he is patient with us, not wishing that anyone should perish, but that all should come to repentance.

Hebrews 10:37

[37] "In a very little while, he who comes will come, and will not wait.

7 * * *

Matthew 24:14

[14] This Good News of the Kingdom will be preached in the whole world for a testimony to all the nations, and then the end will come.

8 * * *

Luke 18:7

[7] Won't God avenge his chosen ones who are crying out to him day and night, and yet he exercises patience with them?

Colossians 3:12

¹² Put on therefore, as God's chosen ones, holy and beloved, a heart of compassion, kindness, lowliness, humility, and perseverance;

Romans 8:28-30

²⁸ We know that all things work together for good for those who love God, for those who are called according to his purpose. ²⁹ For whom he foreknew, he also predestined to be conformed to the image of his Son, that he might be the firstborn among many brothers. (The word for "brothers" here and where context allows may also be correctly translated "brothers and sisters" or "siblings.") ³⁰ Whom he predestined, those he also called. Whom he called, those he also justified. Whom he justified, those he also glorified.

₉ * * *

Daniel 9:26-27

²⁶ After the sixty-two weeks the Anointed One ("Anointed One" can also be translated "Messiah" - same as "Christ".) will be cut off, and will have nothing. The people of the prince who come will destroy the city and the sanctuary. Its end will be with a flood, and war will be even to the end. Desolations are determined. ²⁷ He will make a firm covenant with many for one week. In the middle of the week he will cause the sacrifice and the offering to cease. On the wing of abominations will come one who makes desolate; and even to the full end, and that determined, wrath will be poured out on the desolate."

Matthew 24:15-22

¹⁵ "When, therefore, you see the abomination of desolation, which was spoken of through Daniel the prophet, standing in the holy place (let the reader understand), ¹⁶ then let those who are in Judea flee to the mountains. ¹⁷ Let him who is on the housetop not go down to take out the things that are in his house. ¹⁸ Let him who is in the field not return back to get his clothes. ¹⁹ But woe to those who are with child and to nursing mothers in those days! ²⁰ Pray that your flight will not be in the winter nor on a Sabbath, ²¹ for then there will be great suffering, (or, oppression) such as has not been from the beginning of the world until now, no, nor ever will be. ²² Unless those days had been shortened, no flesh would have

been saved. But for the sake of the chosen ones, those days will be shortened.

1 Thessalonians 5:1-3
But concerning the times and the seasons, brothers, you have no need that anything be written to you. 2 For you yourselves know well that the day of the Lord comes like a thief in the night. 3 For when they are saying, "Peace and safety," then sudden destruction will come on them, like birth pains on a pregnant woman. Then they will in no way escape.

Revelation 6:1-8
I saw that the Lamb opened one of the seven seals, and I heard one of the four living creatures saying, as with a voice of thunder, "Come and see!" 2 Then a white horse appeared, and he who sat on it had a bow. A crown was given to him, and he came out conquering, and to conquer. 3 When he opened the second seal, I heard the second living creature saying, "Come!" 4 Another came out: a red horse. To him who sat on it was given power to take peace from the earth, and that they should kill one another. There was given to him a great sword. 5 When he opened the third seal, I heard the third living creature saying, "Come and see!" And behold, a black horse, and he who sat on it had a balance in his hand. 6 I heard a voice in the middle of the four living creatures saying, "A choenix (A choenix is a dry volume measure that is a little more than a liter (a little more than a quart).) of wheat for a denarius, and three choenix of barley for a denarius! Don't damage the oil and the wine!" 7 When he opened the fourth seal, I heard the fourth living creature saying, "Come and see!" 8 And behold, a pale horse, and the name of he who sat on it was Death. Hades (or, Hell) followed with him. Authority over one fourth of the earth, to kill with the sword, with famine, with death, and by the wild animals of the earth was given to him.

10 * * *
Daniel 7:19-23
19 "Then I desired to know the truth concerning the fourth animal, which was different from all of them, exceedingly terrible, whose teeth were of iron, and its nails of bronze; which devoured, broke

138

in pieces, and stamped the residue with its feet; 20 and concerning the ten horns that were on its head, and the other horn which came up, and before which three fell, even that horn that had eyes, and a mouth that spoke great things, whose look was more stout than its fellows. 21 I saw, and the same horn made war with the saints, and prevailed against them, 22 until the ancient of days came, and judgment was given to the saints of the Most High, and the time came that the saints possessed the kingdom.

23 "So he said, 'The fourth animal will be a fourth kingdom on earth, which will be different from all the kingdoms, and will devour the whole earth, and will tread it down, and break it in pieces.

Daniel 8:23-25
23 "In the latter time of their kingdom, when the transgressors have come to the full, a king of fierce face, and understanding dark sentences, will stand up. 24 His power will be mighty, but not by his own power. He will destroy awesomely, and will prosper in what he does. He will destroy the mighty ones and the holy people. 25 Through his policy he will cause deceit to prosper in his hand. He will magnify himself in his heart, and he will destroy many in their security. He will also stand up against the prince of princes; but he will be broken without hand.

Revelation 13:1-7
Then I stood on the sand of the sea. I saw a beast coming up out of the sea, having ten horns and seven heads. On his horns were ten crowns, and on his heads, blasphemous names. 2 The beast which I saw was like a leopard, and his feet were like those of a bear, and his mouth like the mouth of a lion. The dragon gave him his power, his throne, and great authority. 3 One of his heads looked like it had been wounded fatally. His fatal wound was healed, and the whole earth marveled at the beast. 4 They worshiped the dragon, because he gave his authority to the beast, and they worshiped the beast, saying, "Who is like the beast? Who is able to make war with him?" 5 A mouth speaking great things and blasphemy was given to him. Authority to make war for forty-two months was given to him. 6 He opened his mouth for blasphemy against God, to blaspheme his name, and his dwelling,

those who dwell in heaven. ⁷ It was given to him to make war with the saints, and to overcome them. Authority over every tribe, people, language, and nation was given to him.

11 * * *

Revelation 13:11-18
¹¹ I saw another beast coming up out of the earth. He had two horns like a lamb, and he spoke like a dragon. ¹² He exercises all the authority of the first beast in his presence. He makes the earth and those who dwell in it to worship the first beast, whose fatal wound was healed. ¹³ He performs great signs, even making fire come down out of the sky to the earth in the sight of people. ¹⁴ He deceives my own people who dwell on the earth because of the signs he was granted to do in front of the beast, saying to those who dwell on the earth that they should make an image to the beast who had the sword wound and lived. ¹⁵ It was given to him to give breath to it, to the image of the beast, that the image of the beast should both speak, and cause as many as wouldn't worship the image of the beast to be killed. ¹⁶ He causes all, the small and the great, the rich and the poor, and the free and the slave, to be given marks on their right hands, or on their foreheads; ¹⁷ and that no one would be able to buy or to sell, unless he has that mark, which is the name of the beast or the number of his name. ¹⁸ Here is wisdom. He who has understanding, let him calculate the number of the beast, for it is the number of a man. His number is six hundred sixty-six.

Revelation 17:1-6
One of the seven angels who had the seven bowls came and spoke with me, saying, "Come here. I will show you the judgment of the great prostitute who sits on many waters, ² with whom the kings of the earth committed sexual immorality. Those who dwell in the earth were made drunken with the wine of her sexual immorality." ³ He carried me away in the Spirit into a wilderness. I saw a woman sitting on a scarlet-colored beast, full of blasphemous names, having seven heads and ten horns. ⁴ The woman was dressed in purple and scarlet, and decked with gold and precious stones and pearls, having in her hand a golden cup full of abominations and the impurities of the sexual immorality

of the earth. 5 And on her forehead a name was written, "MYSTERY, BABYLON THE GREAT, THE MOTHER OF THE PROSTITUTES AND OF THE ABOMINATIONS OF THE EARTH." 6 I saw the woman drunken with the blood of the saints, and with the blood of the martyrs of Jesus. When I saw her, I wondered with great amazement.

12 * * *

Revelation 13:11-12
11 I saw another beast coming up out of the earth. He had two horns like a lamb, and he spoke like a dragon. 12 He exercises all the authority of the first beast in his presence. He makes the earth and those who dwell in it to worship the first beast, whose fatal wound was healed.

13 * * *

Daniel 11:36
36 "The king will do according to his will. He will exalt himself, and magnify himself above every god, and will speak marvelous things against the God of gods. He will prosper until the indignation is accomplished; for that which is determined will be done.

2 Thessalonians 2:3-4
3 Let no one deceive you in any way. For it will not be, unless the rebellion (or, *falling away*, or, *defection*) comes first, and the man of sin is revealed, the son of destruction, 4 he who opposes and exalts himself against all that is called God or that is worshiped, so that he sits as God in the temple of God, setting himself up as God.

14 * * *

Revelation 6:12-17
12 I saw when he opened the sixth seal, and there was a great earthquake. The sun became black as sackcloth made of hair, and the whole moon became as blood. 13 The stars of the sky fell to the earth, like a fig tree dropping its unripe figs when it is shaken by a great wind. 14 The sky was removed like a scroll when it is rolled up. Every mountain and island was moved out of its place. 15 The kings of the earth, the princes, the commanding officers, the rich, the strong, and every slave and free person, hid themselves in the

caves and in the rocks of the mountains. [16] They told the mountains and the rocks, "Fall on us, and hide us from the face of him who sits on the throne, and from the wrath of the Lamb, [17] for the great day of his wrath has come; and who is able to stand?"

Revelation 11:15
[15] The seventh angel sounded, and great voices in heaven followed, saying, "The kingdom of the world has become the Kingdom of our Lord, and of his Christ. He will reign forever and ever!"

Revelation 11:19
[19] God's temple that is in heaven was opened, and the ark of the Lord's covenant was seen in his temple. Lightnings, sounds, thunders, an earthquake, and great hail followed.

Revelation 15:1
I saw another great and marvelous sign in the sky: seven angels having the seven last plagues, for in them God's wrath is finished.

Revelation 16:1-4
I heard a loud voice out of the temple, saying to the seven angels, "Go and pour out the seven bowls of the wrath of God on the earth!" [2] The first went, and poured out his bowl into the earth, and it became a harmful and evil sore on the people who had the mark of the beast, and who worshiped his image. [3] The second angel poured out his bowl into the sea, and it became blood as of a dead man. Every living thing in the sea died. [4] The third poured out his bowl into the rivers and springs of water, and they became blood.

Revelation 16:8-10
[8] The fourth poured out his bowl on the sun, and it was given to him to scorch men with fire. [9] People were scorched with great heat, and people blasphemed the name of God who has the power over these plagues. They didn't repent and give him glory. [10] The fifth poured out his bowl on the throne of the beast, and his kingdom was darkened. They gnawed their tongues because of the pain,

15 * * *

Revelation 17:15-18

15 He said to me, "The waters which you saw, where the prostitute sits, are peoples, multitudes, nations, and languages. 16 The ten horns which you saw, and the beast, these will hate the prostitute, will make her desolate, will strip her naked, will eat her flesh, and will burn her utterly with fire. 17 For God has put in their hearts to do what he has in mind, to be of one mind, and to give their kingdom to the beast, until the words of God should be accomplished. 18 The woman whom you saw is the great city, which reigns over the kings of the earth."

16 * * *

1 Thessalonians 4:13-18

13 But we don't want you to be ignorant, brothers, concerning those who have fallen asleep, so that you don't grieve like the rest, who have no hope. 14 For if we believe that Jesus died and rose again, even so God will bring with him those who have fallen asleep in Jesus. 15 For this we tell you by the word of the Lord, that we who are alive, who are left until the coming of the Lord, will in no way precede those who have fallen asleep. 16 For the Lord himself will descend from heaven with a shout, with the voice of the archangel and with God's trumpet. The dead in Christ will rise first, 17 then we who are alive, who are left, will be caught up together with them in the clouds, to meet the Lord in the air. So we will be with the Lord forever. 18 Therefore comfort one another with these words.

Revelation 3:10

10 Because you kept my command to endure, I also will keep you from the hour of testing which is to come on the whole world, to test those who dwell on the earth.

17 * * *

Matthew 7:14

14 How the gate is narrow and the way is restricted that leads to life! There are who find it.

2 Thessalonians 2:9-12
9 even he whose coming is according to the working of Satan with all power and signs and lying wonders, 10 and with all deception of wickedness for those who are being lost, because they didn't receive the love of the truth, that they might be saved. 11 Because of this, God sends them a working of error, that they should believe a lie; 12 that they all might be judged who didn't believe the truth, but had pleasure in unrighteousness.

18 * * *

Daniel 9:27
27 He will make a firm covenant with many for one week. In the middle of the week he will cause the sacrifice and the offering to cease. On the wing of abominations will come one who makes desolate; and even to the full end, and that determined, wrath will be poured out on the desolate."

2 Thessalonians 2:3
3 Let no one deceive you in any way. For it will not be, unless the rebellion (or, *falling away*, or, *defection*) comes first, and the man of sin is revealed, the son of destruction,

2 Thessalonians 2:8
8 Then the lawless one will be revealed, whom the Lord will kill with the breath of his mouth, and destroy by the manifestation of his coming;

19 * * *

Mark 13:24-26
24 But in those days, after that oppression, the sun will be darkened, the moon will not give its light, 25 the stars will be falling from the sky, and the powers that are in the heavens will be shaken. 26 Then they will see the Son of Man coming in clouds with great power and glory.

Luke 21:25-27
25 There will be signs in the sun, moon, and stars; and on the earth anxiety of nations, in perplexity for the roaring of the sea and the waves; 26 men fainting for fear, and for expectation of the things

---

which are coming on the world: for the powers of the heavens will be shaken. [27] Then they will see the Son of Man coming in a cloud with power and great glory.

Acts 1:10-11
[10] While they were looking steadfastly into the sky as he went, behold, two men stood by them in white clothing, [11] who also said, "You men of Galilee, why do you stand looking into the sky? This Jesus, who was received up from you into the sky, will come back in the same way as you saw him going into the sky."

Revelation 22:20
[20] He who testifies these things says, "Yes, I come quickly." Amen! Yes, come, Lord Jesus.

[20] * * *

Matthew 1:21
[21] She shall give birth to a son. You shall name him Jesus, ("Jesus" means "Salvation") for it is he who shall save his people from their sins."

Luke 2:14
[14] "Glory to God in the highest, on earth peace, good will toward men."

Luke 2:29-32
[29] "Now you are releasing your servant, Master, according to your word, in peace; [30] for my eyes have seen your salvation [31]which you have prepared before the face of all peoples; [32] a light for revelation to the nations, and the glory of your people Israel."

John 12:47
[47] If anyone listens to my sayings, and doesn't believe, I don't judge him. For I came not to judge the world, but to save the world.

Titus 2:11
[11] For the grace of God has appeared, bringing salvation to all men,

[21] * * *

John 12:48-50
⁴⁸ He who rejects me, and doesn't receive my sayings, has one who judges him. The word that I spoke will judge him in the last day. ⁴⁹ For I spoke not from myself, but the Father who sent me, he gave me a commandment, what I should say, and what I should speak. ⁵⁰ I know that his commandment is eternal life. The things therefore which I speak, even as the Father has said to me, so I speak."

Hebrews 10:30-31
³⁰ For we know him who said, "Vengeance belongs to me. I will repay," says the Lord. Again, "The Lord will judge his people." ³¹ It is a fearful thing to fall into the hands of the living God.

22 * * *

Joel 3:1-3
"For, behold, in those days, and in that time, when I restore the fortunes of Judah and Jerusalem, ² I will gather all nations, and will bring them down into the valley of Jehoshaphat; and I will execute judgment on them there for my people, and for my heritage, Israel, whom they have scattered among the nations. They have divided my land, ³ and have cast lots for my people, and have given a boy for a prostitute, and sold a girl for wine, that they may drink.

Zechariah 12:1-6 (ESV)
¹ The oracle of the word of the LORD concerning Israel: Thus declares the LORD, who stretched out the heavens and founded the earth and formed the spirit of man within him: ² "Behold, I am about to make Jerusalem a cup of staggering to all the surrounding peoples. The siege of Jerusalem will also be against Judah. ³ On that day I will make Jerusalem a heavy stone for all the peoples. All who lift it will surely hurt themselves. And all the nations of the earth will gather against it. ⁴ On that day, declares the LORD, I will strike every horse with panic, and its rider with madness. But for the sake of the house of Judah I will keep my eyes open, when I strike every horse of the peoples with blindness. ⁵ Then the clans of Judah shall say to themselves, 'The inhabitants of Jerusalem have strength through the LORD of hosts, their God.' ⁶

"On that day I will make the clans of Judah like a blazing pot in the midst of wood, like a flaming torch among sheaves. And they shall devour to the right and to the left all the surrounding peoples, while Jerusalem shall again be inhabited in its place, in Jerusalem.

23 * * *

Zechariah 12:10-11

10 I will pour on David's house, and on the inhabitants of Jerusalem, the spirit of grace and of supplication; and they will look to me whom they have pierced; and they shall mourn for him, as one mourns for his only son, and will grieve bitterly for him, as one grieves for his firstborn. 11 In that day there will be a great mourning in Jerusalem, like the mourning of Hadadrimmon in the valley of Megiddon.

Zechariah 13:8-9 (ESV)

8 In the whole land, declares the LORD, two thirds shall be cut off and perish, and one third shall be left alive. 9 And I will put this third into the fire, and refine them as one refines silver, and test them as gold is tested. They will call upon my name, and I will answer them. I will say, 'They are my people'; and they will say, 'The LORD is my God.'"

Zechariah 14:2

2 For I will gather all nations against Jerusalem to battle; and the city will be taken, the houses rifled, and the women ravished. Half of the city will go out into captivity, and the rest of the people will not be cut off from the city.

Luke 13:34-35

34 "Jerusalem, Jerusalem, you who kills the prophets and stones those who are sent to her! How often I wanted to gather your children together, like a hen gathers her own brood under her wings, and you refused! 35 Behold, your house is left to you desolate. I tell you, you will not see me until you say, 'Blessed is he who comes in the name of the Lord!'"

24 * * *

Zechariah 14:5 (ESV) _____

5 And you shall flee to the valley of my mountains, for the valley of the mountains shall reach to Azal. And you shall flee as you fled from the earthquake in the days of Uzziah king of Judah. Then the LORD my God will come, and all the holy ones with him.

Revelation 17:14
14 These will war against the Lamb, and the Lamb will overcome them, for he is Lord of lords, and King of kings, and those who are with him are called chosen and faithful."

25 * * *

Daniel 2:44
44 "In the days of those kings the God of heaven will set up a kingdom which will never be destroyed, nor will its sovereignty be left to another people; but it will break in pieces and consume all these kingdoms, and it will stand forever.

Revelation 16:12-16
12 The sixth poured out his bowl on the great river, the Euphrates. Its water was dried up, that the way might be prepared for the kings that come from the sunrise. 13 I saw coming out of the mouth of the dragon, and out of the mouth of the beast, and out of the mouth of the false prophet, three unclean spirits, something like frogs; 14 for they are spirits of demons, performing signs; which go out to the kings of the whole inhabited earth, to gather them together for the war of that great day of God, the Almighty. 15 "Behold, I come like a thief. Blessed is he who watches, and keeps his clothes, so that he doesn't walk naked, and they see his shame." 16 He gathered them together into the place which is called in Hebrew, "Megiddo".

Revelation 19:19-21
19 I saw the beast, and the kings of the earth, and their armies, gathered together to make war against him who sat on the horse, and against his army. 20 The beast was taken, and with him the false prophet who worked the signs in his sight, with which he deceived those who had received the mark of the beast and those who worshiped his image. These two were thrown alive into the lake of fire that burns with sulfur. 21 The rest were killed with the

sword of him who sat on the horse, the sword which came out of his mouth. So all the birds were filled with their flesh.

Revelation 20:1-3

I saw an angel coming down out of heaven, having the key of the abyss and a great chain in his hand. 2 He seized the dragon, the old serpent, which is the devil and Satan, who deceives the whole inhabited earth, and bound him for a thousand years, 3 and cast him into the abyss, and shut it, and sealed it over him, that he should deceive the nations no more, until the thousand years were finished. After this, he must be freed for a short time.

26 * * *

Isaiah 2:1-5 (ESV)

1 The word that Isaiah the son of Amoz saw concerning Judah and Jerusalem. 2 It shall come to pass in the latter days that the mountain of the house of the LORD shall be established as the highest of the mountains, and shall be lifted up above the hills; and all the nations shall flow to it, 3 and many peoples shall come, and say: "Come, let us go up to the mountain of the LORD, to the house of the God of Jacob, that he may teach us his ways and that we may walk in his paths." For out of Zion shall go the law, and the word of the LORD from Jerusalem. 4 He shall judge between the nations, and shall decide disputes for many peoples; and they shall beat their swords into plowshares, and their spears into pruning hooks; nation shall not lift up sword against nation, neither shall they learn war anymore. 5 O house of Jacob, come, let us walk in the light of the LORD.

Matthew 24:29-31

29 "But immediately after the suffering (or, oppression) of those days, the sun will be darkened, the moon will not give its light, the stars will fall from the sky, and the powers of the heavens will be shaken; 30 and then the sign of the Son of Man will appear in the sky. Then all the tribes of the earth will mourn, and they will see the Son of Man coming on the clouds of the sky with power and great glory. 31 He will send out his angels with a great sound of a trumpet, and they will gather together his chosen ones from the four winds, from one end of the sky to the other.

Revelation 20:4-6

4 I saw thrones, and they sat on them, and judgment was given to them. I saw the souls of those who had been beheaded for the testimony of Jesus, and for the word of God, and such as didn't worship the beast nor his image, and didn't receive the mark on their forehead and on their hand. They lived and reigned with Christ for a thousand years. 5 The rest of the dead didn't live until the thousand years were finished. This is the first resurrection. 6 Blessed and holy is he who has part in the first resurrection. Over these, the second death has no power, but they will be priests of God and of Christ, and will reign with him one thousand years.

27 * * *

Revelation 20:7-10

7 And after the thousand years, Satan will be released from his prison, 8 and he will come out to deceive the nations which are in the four corners of the earth, Gog and Magog, to gather them together to the war; the number of whom is as the sand of the sea. 9 They went up over the width of the earth, and surrounded the camp of the saints, and the beloved city. Fire came down out of heaven from God and devoured them. 10 The devil who deceived them was thrown into the lake of fire and sulfur, where the beast and the false prophet are also. They will be tormented day and night forever and ever.

28 * * *

John 5:28-29

28 Don't marvel at this, for the hour comes in which all who are in the tombs will hear his voice, 29 and will come out; those who have done good, to the resurrection of life; and those who have done evil, to the resurrection of judgment.

Revelation 20:11-15

11 I saw a great white throne, and him who sat on it, from whose face the earth and the heaven fled away. There was found no place for them. 12 I saw the dead, the great and the small, standing before the throne, and they opened books. Another book was opened,

which is the book of life. The dead were judged out of the things which were written in the books, according to their works. [13] The sea gave up the dead who were in it. Death and Hades (or, Hell) gave up the dead who were in them. They were judged, each one according to his works. [14] Death and Hades (or, Hell) were thrown into the lake of fire. This is the second death, the lake of fire. [15] If anyone was not found written in the book of life, he was cast into the lake of fire.

Revelation 21:8
[8] But for the cowardly, unbelieving, sinners, abominable, murderers, sexually immoral, sorcerers, (The word for "sorcerers" here also includes users of potions and drugs.) idolaters, and all liars, their part is in the lake that burns with fire and sulfur, which is the second death."

29 * * *

Isaiah 65:17
[17] "For, behold, I create new heavens and a new earth; and the former things will not be remembered, nor come into mind.

Revelation 21:1-7
I saw a new heaven and a new earth: for the first heaven and the first earth have passed away, and the sea is no more. [2] I saw the holy city, New Jerusalem, coming down out of heaven from God, prepared like a bride adorned for her husband. [3] I heard a loud voice out of heaven saying, "Behold, God's dwelling is with people, and he will dwell with them, and they will be his people, and God himself will be with them as their God. [4] He will wipe away every tear from their eyes. Death will be no more; neither will there be mourning, nor crying, nor pain, any more. The first things have passed away." [5] He who sits on the throne said, "Behold, I am making all things new." He said, "Write, for these words of God are faithful and true." [6] He said to me, "I am the Alpha and the Omega, the Beginning and the End. I will give freely to him who is thirsty from the spring of the water of life. [7] He who overcomes, I will give him these things. I will be his God, and he will be my son.

Revelation 22:12-14

[12] "Behold, I come quickly. My reward is with me, to repay to each man according to his work. [13] I am the Alpha and the Omega, the First and the Last, the Beginning and the End. [14] Blessed are those who do his commandments, that they may have the right to the tree of life, and may enter in by the gates into the city.

Chapter 11

THE MOST ESSENTIAL TRUTH

What you have read is what I would prefer to have told you in person, if life would only afford us the time to examine such things. Of course, if that were the case, then I would have also been challenged to present it to you in a coherent way. Only then might you feel compelled to seize it to the point of action. This book is an attempt to overcome both of those challenges so that you may ponder the details and grasp the seriousness of the subject. Chances are that in your lifetime you have already been exposed to some of what has been written, but perhaps as you weigh a broader perspective, it may begin to gel in your heart in a greater way. I entrust you to the Holy Spirit for that.

Look for the Big Picture

My unabashed hope is that you will come away from this exercise with a fine-tuned perspective on life. If we allow ourselves to be duped into thinking that there is little or no merit to valuing spiritual things, then all we've done is decided to walk blindly through this world. With heads down, focused on today's business and preparing for tomorrow's, we miss the big picture. Almost equally treacherous is to assume that our limited spiritual understanding is adequate to meet the demands for eternity. Such foolish complacency may prove to be as destructive as total ignorance.

How little is the benefit to be gained by a one-hundred-year life filled with activities and ending in death, in comparison to those same years spent with God-given focus, followed by a life in eternity with untold wonders. The first makes little sense; the second paints a far more intelligent picture and raises the question of how to aspire to it. Ignorance leaves one feeling hopeless and helpless to change things, and so oftentimes spiritual things are relegated to the background at best. Yet, as you have read, that is not God's way or His desire. He has provided all that anyone needs to see beyond the natural and the immediate, into His own perspective, plans and strategies. The wise will come into alignment with Him.

The Creation Reflects God's Glory

Now I know that some who read these words are still of the mindset that God does not even exist, therefore there is nothing and no one to align with. If you are in that small percentage of people who call themselves atheists, and you have read through to this point with an open heart and an open mind, you are to be commended. Whatever your motivation, if you examine the references given, you just may find that you begin to see things differently. You certainly would not be the first atheist to come to faith in God; so perhaps it would help you to research their lives as well.

Aside from that however, for all readers, may I suggest that the existence of a Creator God is the simplest, most logical and easiest to believe explanation for this world of ours? Consider human bodies composed of multiple, intricate, highly-engineered and interdependent systems; wildlife and plant life with their own complexities; this entire Earth system designed to contain it all. I know little about any of those things, but I am amazed by all of it. And that's not even to begin to speak of the beauty found throughout. Even in its fallen state it is a breathtaking masterpiece which begs the existence of a Creator.

What other explanation can hold any merit? Evolution? That somehow there was a big bang and something came into existence; and then over billions of years that one little speck evolved into all we see today? I think in today's world even most scientists have a hard time believing such a thing is conceivable. I have heard it said before that it would take a far greater faith to believe in Evolution than to believe in God, and I wholeheartedly agree with that.

There is One True God

Now for all those who profess belief in God there is still the potentially confusing issue of different "gods" for different religions. Many will say that's not a problem; most likely the same god, just a different name or a different way to worship; no harm done. But I hasten to say that that is indeed a problem so long as anyone is being led along a wrong path. Blind acceptance, blind faith, trust in a man's word - all are closed-minded efforts to grasp at truth. Again, the long history of the Israelite nation makes clear the futility of trusting in false gods.

Then too, there is the inexhaustible ability of man to assign attributes to God of his own choosing, thereby fashioning a god he is most comfortable with. The only rock-solid way to go is the one laid out by the One True God. Two millennia ago, God sent His only Son to establish the one way acceptable to Him. The birth, life, death, resurrection and ascension back into heaven of Jesus, the Christ, is a matter of undeniable history. Clearly, the sacrifice made was God's magnanimous sign of His love for mankind and His desire for reconciliation. Jesus willingly paid the price, the Way was made, and to presume that any other way is acceptable or effective is just more deception. How could the Father sacrifice His Son specifically for the salvation of mankind, and then approve of any other alternative? That should be preposterous even to the uninformed mind.

Truth is Revealed by the Spirit of God

No doubt there are those still who will contend that since all here is based on the Holy Bible, then it has no merit because the Bible itself is unreliable. Many others have written on both sides of that argument and of course you can do your own research, but I would encourage you not to spend your time that way. It might make for an interesting intellectual diversion, but I must reemphasize that clear understanding and appreciation of the Scriptures will only come through the counsel of the Holy Spirit. Detailed scholarly analysis in the natural by even the greatest minds will never compare to the riches to be revealed spiritually by the Spirit. And the Holy Spirit will only be given with the softening of one's heart to God and the acceptance of Jesus by faith, as the Father draws you to Him. The best I can suggest is to ask for God's mercy in that process. That will be the best place to apply your time and energy. Myself and others are praying for you.

Of course, the fact is that all here is not based simply on biblical analysis and interpretation. Certainly, the facts are founded in the Scriptures, but the understanding is hereby testified to personally as accurate and rich with meaning, provided by the graciousness of the Holy Spirit. The spiritual reality of what has been written is alive beyond a doubt in my own life. I absolutely must share this information with whomever is open to it. Even if I was the richest and most powerful person on Earth, there is nothing better that I could give to anyone.

One Essential Truth

Now there have been many truths put forth in this book, all of which I hope have been helpful. However, at the risk of being redundant, there is *one essential truth* which is most important. Specifically, you don't have to take a word of what has been written as truth, because you have the option of finding out for yourself. In fact, you don't have to blindly accept the words of anyone who promotes any doctrine, because the Way that has been made enables everyone to go right to the Source for understanding. You can be born again by the Spirit of God and begin to learn the Truth. The only question is if you are willing. If you seek Him, you will find Him. The obstacles may be many and even challenging to overcome, but it all begins in your heart, speaking directly to the heart of God. That is very simple and totally within your control. Don't put it off, because then you must accept responsibility for having made a choice for which you may be very sorry. May the love of God pierce through every barrier so that His light shines brightly in your life.

Chapter 12

CONNECTING WITH THE SPIRITUAL

Hopefully by now you have been at least somewhat persuaded that the realm of the spiritual things of God is well within your reach. God truly is with us and is more than willing to see us through this life. The Way that He has made is not some cryptic dogma shrouded in mystery that only some elite holy men can even hope to understand. I am not a theologian or a scholar of any type, and like many others I am always learning. Still, I am very confident in what I have learned and have written. Additionally, I see that there are many like myself, not necessarily professionally schooled, but primarily blessed by the Word of God and guided by the Holy Spirit.

This Way is not a theory concocted by man; it is not a religion founded on doctrine without reality; it is not a road to follow with blind faith and it certainly does not foster blind hope in spiritual mysteries. On the contrary, this Way is God's preplanned strategy which is plain and simple and available to all. And it is a living Way, not one based on empty words of ancient manuscripts, because it is centered in the life of the very Son of God, Jesus Christ. Connecting with God is what it's all about. This is where you will find the union of the natural with the spiritual. This is where the meaning of life begins to take shape.

Be Prepared for Obstacles

Now if you really want to get to that place of truly and clearly seeing beyond the things of life in the natural, then you should also anticipate that there likely will be barriers to overcome. You will need to arrive at that point of choice where you say "yes" to God's Way and there can be any number of obstacles along the way. I have said it before but I will reemphasize that although the mind should be fully engaged, this effort is more importantly one of the heart and of the supernatural.

So, for example, anything that has emotionally clogged the heart may be a problem, such as upset or bitterness over the loss of a loved one or a job. Any of the many life events that can leave wounds and scars can also leave one in a place of doubt or even opposition to God. Also, some people are so locked in to a specific formal religion through family roots that they absolutely refuse to even consider a thought beyond what they know. Of course, self-centeredness or self-sufficiency are horrible traps because they simply exclude God from the picture. And complacency can be a real killer, putting off important decisions to a tomorrow that may not arrive. The list of life circumstances that can get in your way is endless. And then of course there are those evil spiritual beings who labor without rest to keep you from God.

Don't Let Obstacles Stop You

For the person with a sincere heart to press through every barrier, there is no obstacle that is impossible to overcome. The range of opposition may be quite wide from one person to the next, but even those on the extreme end of difficulty can find peace with God. It is very important to note that any roadblock does not have to be totally removed in order to move on. Sometimes all that is necessary is to go around it, then later God will work with you to clean up whatever mess may be there.

In other words, make a heart-felt decision not to let any obstacle keep you from getting to the Truth. Whatever it is you can lay it out before God, telling Him that you know there's an issue and you want it to be different, even though you have no idea how to make it happen. Hunger and search for the Truth and God will make sure that you get there. In a similar vein, don't let your lack of understanding on any particular point slow your progress. Intellectual comprehension should not be your primary objective. As previously stated, without the Holy Spirit it is not even possible to truly comprehend spiritual matters. Therefore, if your heart is telling you to accept something and move on, don't let your mind get in the way. If it's a major issue God will help you deal with it right away, and if not, trust that He will make things clearer for you at the appropriate time.

Be Straight with God

With every step that you take on this spiritual journey be certain to always be totally open and honest with God. He knows you personally whether or not you know Him at all. He not only sees your every action and hears your every spoken word, He also knows your thoughts, what is going on in your heart and even the motivations for your actions. That may be difficult to hear and to comprehend and to believe, but it is very true. Therefore, it only makes sense to be transparent in your dealings with Him. So, even if you hate Him or doubt His existence or find pleasure in things you know offend Him, He already knows it all so you won't surprise Him by being honest. All your cards are already on the table so to speak, and He would just like to help you deal with them.

God cannot be fooled, so never attempt to proceed like you're taking out an insurance policy for everlasting life. That's what I did in my early years and that's what many people are doing today, whether they know it or not, when they automatically follow the rituals of a religion. God hates that. He wants you to join Him in love and in heart which is far from some kind of religious contract. He will value your sincerity as precious, and He will deal with your insincerity as a good Father.

Be Open to His Leading

Once you have set your mind and your will and your heart to be open to God, then you will want to be sensitive to what He does to lead you spiritually. It is the Father who draws people to Jesus, so you want to stay open to His leading and respond accordingly. That may be something as simple as feeling the desire to look deeper into even a single point that you read here. As you follow through, you will be blessed. Ideally, someone who cares about your life will have given you a copy of this book. That person might then be a primary resource for you to discuss things with. Whether that is an option for you or not, if you find yourself to still be in a place of uncertainty, then talk to God about what is specifically a concern or hindrance for you. As always, it is best to just use your own words, and be as specific as you can be, but for anyone who may want some help you can say the following:

God, I need your help. I have read these words and I have looked into the references in your Holy Bible. Still, I find that I remain uncertain about some things and so I'm hesitant to go any further. I am asking you to help me get these things clarified in my heart, because if nothing else, I know that I want to be right with you. So please help me to sort through these issues so that I can get to a place of certainty rather than confusion. Thank you.

Always be open to however God will provide you with directions. Don't be waiting to hear an audible voice because it seems that that rarely happens. But there are many ways God will get through to you with what you need. That may be through a greater understanding while reading the Bible. It may also be by the Holy Spirit guiding your spirit to a specific section in the Bible. Many references have been provided in this book to give you a good start on many subjects. Check them out for yourself, especially those areas that are the vaguest in your mind. Those references have been intentionally limited to provide focus on the key points, but you may find it very helpful to read the Scriptures which precede and / or follow the ones noted, in order to get the fuller context.

Oftentimes God will use other people to guide you, whether it's with a book, or a podcast, or just a simple comment. Don't give up until you get what you need. God will be with you through it all. Trust that He has your best at heart. No matter what method He uses to lead you, you will have a confidence in your heart because He is gentle and loving and always guiding you into Truth. Your brain and your spirit are connected, so use them together to make wise choices.

Consider the Cost

The honesty, openness and truthfulness of God does not stop when the subject shifts to unpopular ones. That was noted earlier for example on the subject of heaven and hell. When Jesus walked the face of this earth two thousand years ago, His life and His words disrupted the status quo and inflamed hatred in many people; so much so that He was crucified. He didn't pull any punches, as He instructed those who loved and followed Him that they too should expect similar treatment. Things are not any different today. In fact, as we draw closer to the last of the last days, hostility towards the things of God will only grow more intense. So, everyone truly looking to connect with the spiritual should soberly consider that reality before making a greater commitment to the God of creation. That's not to imply that everyone who chooses to follow Jesus will be persecuted to death as He was, yet many have already been, and even today are being treated that harshly.

The costs, the difficult moments, may come with simple life events. For example, it is very common for long-time friendships to be dissolved and even for family relationships to be broken. The decision to live a Godly life may very well cause disruption with those you love who are content with keeping their lives as it is. The changes that you embrace for yourself may simply be unpalatable to them. The truth embodied in Jesus, and which He proclaimed throughout His life, brought a sword to earth, not peace.

That said, it is still true that even among those who have chosen God's Way, there exists varying degrees of commitment. In a regular army some soldiers, by choice, are barely equipped and others are extremely well prepared. Their heart commitment is reflected in their preparedness, and their effectiveness in their job is directly related to their degree of sacrifice. That same principle is at work in God's kingdom. One can choose to remain a dim and flickering flame or to grow in intensity to be a bright light in the world. A poorly-prepared soldier will still have to deal with all the horrors of battle; a weak light is more easily extinguished by the multitude of evil influences that surround us in the world.

Complacency to remain at a low level of preparedness is a less desirable and far more precarious position to be in. So, there is a real cost to be paid, and you can rest assured that at key points along the journey of your life, God will give you the opportunity to count the cost. Whether or not you choose to pay it and make a greater commitment is up to you. Stop at any time and He will love you no less for it. The more you are willing to pay, the closer you will come to fulfilling His highest calling for your life, the greater joy and satisfaction will you experience, and the greater will be your rewards.

Make the Connection

If and when the moment of decision comes to your heart, have no fear, but submit yourself to the mercy of God. You will be in very good hands. If you have had someone knowledgeable about this content to assist you in the process, that person can pray with you and guide you into moving forward in God's Way.

I know that many may not have that assistance for a variety of reasons, so if that is your situation, then just consider these thoughts: Have you read through all these notes and utilized the reference Scriptures as needed? Do you find that it is all speaking to your heart in a positive way, even if you don't fully understand everything? Do you feel in your heart that what you have studied is truthful and makes sense to you? Are you willing to turn away from things that offend God? Are you willing to make a commitment to Him to walk through your life in a way that honors him? And most of all are you feeling compelled in your spirit to make this vital spiritual connection with the God of the universe?

If you still have significant reservations on any of these things, then perhaps today is not the day to move forward. This is strictly between you and God, so don't allow yourself to be overly influenced by anyone to make a decision you are not ready to make. On the other hand, when you can answer "yes" to the heartbeat of those questions, then wait no longer. The grace, faith and motivation to put your trust in Jesus comes from God, not from your own will, so don't hesitate to respond. As always, you can talk to God in your own words, but if you want some assistance you can say the following prayer.

Pray for God to Save You

Father God, my eyes have been opened to see these spiritual matters in a new way and I thank you for it. Honestly, I can't say that I truly understand it all, but I trust that you will help to clarify things for me in the days ahead. Never-the-less, I readily acknowledge that I have sinned and I ask you to forgive me of it all. I see now that without you I have no hope of entering into eternal life. Thank you for sending your son, Jesus Christ, to suffer and die for me. He saved my life by paying the price for my sins and there is nothing I can do to save myself. I decide today to put my faith for entry into your heaven in Jesus' finished work. Please give me your Holy Spirit to be my Helper, delivering me from everything in my life that offends you, and guiding me into the Truth of your Holy Scriptures. Thank you!

The day that you sincerely pray that prayer marks a truly momentous occasion. The Bible says that even the angels in heaven will be rejoicing at that time. Make a note of the date because it is your new spiritual birthday and you will want to remember it always.

Things to Do

Once you have prayed for God's saving grace, you should do everything in your power to grow in wisdom and in your faith. You don't want to remain like that ill-prepared soldier. You have been born again by the Spirit of God and so you start out like a spiritual baby who needs to grow into maturity. Besides the Bible, there is a wealth of resources available which you can draw on when desired. For now, just make note of consistently following up with a few key items:

First, always pray to / talk to God about everything; He is always with you. The Holy Spirit will most gladly counsel you through all of life. First and foremost, follow His leading, which will always flow in the direction of God's purpose for your life. You can be sure that you are being led by the Holy Spirit (and not some demonic spirit) if you are being led in a way that is consistent with the Word of God as found in the Bible.

Second, read and study the Holy Bible consistently. Every time, before you begin reading, pray that the Holy Spirit would open your spiritual eyes to see and your heart to receive. Always look to apply what you read to your own life. Being obedient to what is revealed to you is critical to your growth. If the Bible is something new to you, you will soon find that there are many good translations available. There is value in utilizing multiple translations to gain clearer understanding. You can easily research the characteristics of each on the internet. Doing so will also help you to avoid any that may be intentionally misleading.

Third, look to get connected with other born-again believers in Jesus at a local church or perhaps a bible study group. God has placed many people in the Church to be teachers and while you can learn much on your own, your learning experience can be enriched by those God has appointed for that purpose. Be alert and discerning to what

---

167

you hear though, because in the world there are both false teachers and, sincere teachers with some false teachings. Seeking the wise counsel of multiple, qualified people, is Godly wisdom. The Bible is the Word of God so always make that the guiding light in your life. And always default to the Holy Spirit as your perfectly reliable Teacher.

Fourth, sing songs worshipping God. There are many ways to worship God but you will quickly find that this is a powerful way to draw near to Him. Simply put, it is a wonderful way to acknowledge and appreciate His excellence and sovereignty while setting aside your "self" interest. Your local church will have hymns as part of their services but you can praise Him anywhere. Christian radio stations and internet-based services can be a great resource and of course there are many music discs and downloads available for purchase. Most worship songs are proclaiming part of the Scriptures, so even as you honor Him you will be encouraging yourself in the Lord as you sing along.

Ambassadors for Christ

Once you have begun your personal journey with the Lord you can simultaneously begin to serve Him even as you are learning. Granted, you will start off as a baby needing to gradually grow to maturity, but all along the way you will have something to share with others. From the beginning, make it a habit of letting others know of what you have learned so that they too can begin to know the Truth. Do it as the Lord directs, with gentleness and respect.

A major way that you can impact the lives of others even without saying a word, is simply by living a Godly life. A life changed by the hand of God becomes that ever-increasing brighter light that dispels the darkness. And every life joined to the true Church of Jesus Christ results in the growth of His army; an army united and fully equipped to impact the world with His goodness. The time is short so we must not delay.

∞ ∞ ∞ ∞ ∞

"15 ... speaking the truth in love, we are to grow up in every way into him who is the head, into Christ, 16 from whom the whole body, joined and held together by every joint with which it is equipped, when each part is working properly, makes the body grow so that it builds itself up in love." (Ephesians 4:15-16, ESV)

Appendix

With Love from God

My Dear One,

I have watched you all the days of your life and daily I am right by your side. You have often thought and felt that I am removed from the everyday things that encompass your life, yet I see them all. I know that you feel disconnected from me – I feel the same way. And it is from this deep pain and longing in my heart for a better and more intimate relationship with you, that I put these words down on paper now. What I am about to say to you, I have said before; this is certainly nothing new. My hope is that perhaps now, together, we can sort through the things that have kept us apart and come together with our hearts joined as one. And if today is not the day that this will happen then know that I will look to tomorrow. But please don't put me off, because I so desire that things between us would begin to get better even now. Many times you have thought that this is not possible, but in fact it is. You think that you must wait to die before you can begin to know me, but that simply is not true. There are many alive today that have come to me already with open hearts and our relationship is thriving as we draw closer and closer to each other.

I understand that there are many things in the world that have served to keep you from me. Certain of those things we must begin to talk about. To begin with, I know that there are times when you even question my existence. There are those who tell you that I am not real; that if I were real the world would be a better place in which to live. It is so very true that there is much unrighteousness in the world, all of which I detest, but it does not cast a shadow on my presence. If you begin by guarding yourself from distractions and look deep into your heart, you will find a basic certainty of my existence. This is simply because I created you and I reserved that special, primary, exclusive place in your heart for me; that we may share a life together both now and for eternity. My own heart races as I think about the potential of the relationship we can have together. Examine your reflection, and you will see someone not brought to life by chance, but rather you will see the beautiful, complex, body, soul and spirit that I fashioned to be uniquely you. Listen to your heart and you will hear it shout to you that what you see, clearly, is the work of my hand.

Now also take the time to consider all the natural wonders that surround you. Look at the sky with its backdrop of colors, brushed with ever-changing patterns of clouds. Consider the heavens that embrace a multitude of stars and the sun that provides you warmth and lights your day. Begin to grasp the magnitude of the seas that I put in their place and the wide variety of creatures that I created to inhabit them. View with joy the expanse of trees at the peak of their color, the vast assortment of plants and animals and the delicate beauty of the flowers that bring delight and comfort to the moment. Then ponder in your mind and in your heart the integration and balance of all these things together. I blessed you with these treasures to remind you daily of my presence and of my unending love for you. If you can begin at this point, and openly listen to what my creation is saying to you, our relationship will have a solid foundation. If you listen closely, it will tell you of the greatness of my power. If you listen with the ears of your spirit it will tell you how greatly I care about you and how I always provide for you. Understand that you cannot know and comprehend everything immediately, but you certainly can begin. It is this beginning, a desire from your heart for a fresh start, which I look for and long for. And I will tell you this also; if you are truly one of my own, I will not rest until I have seen you through every battle of confusion and you are at peace in my arms.

Yes, I do love you passionately; more than you can even begin to understand at this point. I know that at times you have wanted to have a more tangible connection with me and you have wondered how that could even be possible. You suffer from lack of knowledge which causes you to see me as being distant and unreachable. The dark reality is that many have fought to keep you from the truth. Those who work against you present falsehoods as truth, conceal the truth altogether and present only part of the truth. Consequently there are many like you who want so much more yet do not understand how to grasp it. You wonder why I have not written sooner but I tell you for sure that I have written much. I have called to your heart but you have pushed me to the back of your mind. I said that what I write now is not anything new because all that you need to know has already been set forth in my book. The Scriptures contain all the information you will ever need and tell you in great detail about who I am. The way to go has been set down in writing and it has been communicated in a multitude of ways. The bible contains my words and my words are true and reliable and accessible to all who would make the effort. Hear me now, a way has been made *and has been in place for hundreds of years. When this way is taken you will find that I am very close and very reachable.*

There are many revelations in my book that you can come to know in time, but it is critical for you to better understand some elementary things immediately if you are to make your way back to me. To begin with you must realize that I have a primary enemy who is called the devil, the evil one, or Satan. You do not see him but you see the results of his destructive ways. His objectives are to steal, kill and destroy. At one time he reigned on the earth but I have dethroned him. In the time he has remaining, the evil one and those who serve him work desperately to come against me and all I have created; against who I am and against any who would stand with me. If you choose my righteous and holy ways, then the devil is your enemy as well. If you do not stand with me, you are in fact standing with him. There is no middle ground and you must choose. I tell you, there is a war raging about you which goes far beyond what you see with your eyes and hear with your ears. You need to be aware of this, and you need to decide which side you will be on.

Certainly there are many things in your present life that keep you busy and while some are necessary and others are not, will you allow them to continue to keep you away from me? You strive to apply yourself and make the most of all that you can in life, which is good. But why ignore the one who gave you the ability to do these things? Your skills, your talents, your qualities, all come from me. They are gifts that I have given to you for your provision and your happiness and even for your survival in difficult times. While I want you to use these things I have blessed you with, I do not want you to be consumed by them to the point that you lose your very soul. Yes, in some situations your efforts will bear fruit, but how long will that fruit last?

Find some success in your activities and the evil one will tell you that you don't need me. Experience difficulty in your activities and the same one will tell you that I don't care about you. With all your plans and preparations and hard work in this season, why have you not made plans for eternity? You strive to establish some security and quality of life for maybe a hundred years, while ignoring the fact that you will go on long after your body stops working. You worry about what you can provide for your children and their future, without giving serious consideration to their eternal life. Will you see and accept that there is a much greater perspective to embrace? Are you going to be satisfied with what you can accomplish with only natural abilities in your very brief span of years? Would you not rather come to me and find that you can be empowered spiritually to achieve so much more? There is a far greater, more glorious and everlasting life to be considered. I tell you most definitely there is an enemy of your soul; one who delights in robbing you of all that I desire for you. Will you go on allowing him to manipulate your pride, your sense of self-sufficiency, your complacency and your fears, to keep you from me? I say turn to me today and you will bear fruit that will last. What good does it do to wait until tomorrow?

I know that you sometimes wonder why, if I really do exist, that I do not intervene in the numerous atrocities that occur all over the world. But I tell you that I have already intervened and much of what you see happening is in fact because of my intervention. Too many have lost loved ones because of the foolishness of others and I am one with them in heart-wrenching grief. Many of my people suffer from traumatic injuries and deathly illness and I know their every pain. My heart is burdened with weights of sorrow to see many deprived of bare essentials and I arise in anger as I witness those who horde their wealth and with greedy hearts deviously amass even greater wealth that simply will testify against them. Natural disasters arise that bring great destruction and snatch lives away prematurely and I mourn the death of each and every one. Countless of my people suffer emotional distress and I intimately share in every torment of their soul even as I see the healing answers that lay ahead. My enemy would keep you believing that I am removed from your life situations when the reality is that I am aware of them all and involved in them all. He would keep you thinking that the only hope you have is in what you can do for yourself, while the truth is at your fingertips and you do not see it. My enemy, your enemy, would keep you blinded in ignorance to your death if at all possible. Satan will try everything in his power to keep you from me.

Again I tell you that what I am about to say I have said before. I will tell you plainly so that hopefully you will ponder my words and will come to know that I am at work on your behalf. Today there are many like yourself who have not yet been told the truth, but now my word is going forth to change that. You can come to know me better with the help of those who have drawn close to me already and are serving me now. They will be able to help you in some ways, but I myself will provide you with all that you need. And now I will tell you how to begin following this way that has been made. I will tell you how to start dealing with truth rather than with deception by telling you about my son Jesus, of whom I am so very proud and who I love so greatly.

My creations, the earth as you see it and mankind as you know it, do not exist today as they did at the beginning. This is because the evil one sought to destroy all that was good, and succeeded in stealing the hearts of my people through his deception. Since then my creation has been in a fallen state, much less than what I desired it to be. The pure and precious connection between my children and I was broken and defiled. But Jesus willingly and joyfully agreed to give up the riches and glory he enjoyed with me in heaven to go down to the earth. His purpose was to make things right again by destroying the works of the devil. So Jesus took on the life of a man and I anointed him with the ability to succeed in the power of the Spirit. And succeed he did, even by willingly laying down his life on the cross. He fought the greatest battle ever fought on earth and won. He overcame the absolute worst that the powers of darkness could ever inflict on any man. Even death could not hold him as I raised him from the dead and he is now seated at my right hand, reigning over all the earth. This glory and this power belong to him and to him alone.

My love, understand this now. The victory won by Jesus broke the rule of tyranny of Satan. Jesus' sacrifice overpowered the grip of the evil one on mankind. Jesus Christ, the King of kings, made the way of victory possible for all who would choose to come to me.

And now, today, you have it within your reach to accept what I have done and to return to me. This is because after Jesus came back to me in heaven, I sent the Holy Spirit to complete what remains to be done on the earth through my people. My son laid down his life for you so that now all you have to do is accept this precious gift he has given. Open your heart to him in thanksgiving for what he has done and he will be with you. Humble yourself before him because he accomplished what no other man could ever do. And because of my son's sacrifice you can feel free to come to us just as you are. It doesn't matter whether you think yourself to be better than some or worse than most. The only thing that truly matters is that you are willing to accept Jesus' sacrifice as the only atonement required for the worst you have ever been or the worst you will ever be. Accept the fact that he gave his life for you, so that you *could have eternal life, and he will give you the Holy Spirit to be your counselor every moment of every day. Your spirit will be born again and you will begin a new life of freedom unlike anything you have known thus far. Jesus accomplished what he did as a man; a man enabled by the power of the Holy Spirit to complete what he was sent to do. He obeyed me in all things and was faithful to the end, making the way possible for you not only to have life eternal, but also to be enabled to overcome in this hour. Because Jesus made the way possible, after you receive the Holy Spirit you too can accomplish all that I have purposed for your life. Then, you can work with me to complete what is left to do at this time on earth. It will be my delight to guide you through a time of restoration; equipping you for all that you will do in my name.*

So you see I have indeed intervened. I took great joy in my creation but it became defiled and still groans in anticipation of the day to come. To redeem the world I sent you my son, Jesus, who paid the ultimate price that any man could offer for his friends. My own heart was tormented with grief that shook the world to watch him be humiliated, tortured and killed. I sent you the Holy Spirit who awaits the opportunity to lead you into all truth by illuminating the Scriptures to you. You can be born again by the Spirit and be enabled to overcome even in this day. Jesus' life was given as a once and final sacrifice for all of mankind. For all who will accept his great gift and put their trust in him, eternal life is given. Soon he will return to earth to receive his own and to take his appointed place as King.

So I ask you, will you turn away from me again? Will you reject my words and sadden my heart further? Will you continue to ignore me when I love you so dearly? Will you blindly follow the ways of deception that cloud your heart or will you once and for all time come to the truth and the only way of victory that is found in my son, Jesus? Your natural mind can think through natural things, but it is only with my Spirit that you will be able to comprehend the things of the spirit. Start with your heart and you will begin to understand. Do you want truth? Do you want unconditional love? Do you want peace that goes beyond understanding? Do you want a close and intimate relationship with one in whom you can have absolute trust? In Jesus you will find all that is beautiful and righteous and holy and strong and faithful. Now is the time. Today is the day. Push back the veil of darkness that would stand in your way and come to me. Let no obstacles block your path. Jesus is waiting, patiently, for you. Seek him out and you will surely find him. Embrace him and you will be empowered with the Holy Spirit. Find Jesus, and you will see me. Come, we are waiting.

I have said much, though there is so much more that I would like to tell you. Do not be overwhelmed, do not be afraid, do not be confused, do not even wonder how to begin. I tell you, just come to me; from the privacy of your own heart, in the stillness of your own room. Talk to me and I will meet you and you will know that I am with you.

Love,

Father God

About the Author

For the first 43 years of his life, Robert A. Fusco lived unaware of how the natural and spiritual realms are intertwined by design. While the practice of a formal religion in his earlier years provided some broad-brush insights, it fell far short in clearly bringing those realms together. He spent the latter part of those years mostly ignoring that grand design, only to find out that ignorance is a very bad choice. He grew to realize that failure to seek out and embrace the very elementary dynamics of this world only leaves one poorly equipped to live within it. Now he seeks to help others understand how to begin that process for themselves. He pulls no punches when he states the absolutely critical importance for everyone to "take charge of" their spiritual destiny.

Bob grew up in Cranston, Rhode Island, the state in which he still lives. Following a false start into higher education, Bob served as an electrician in the U.S. Navy Reserve during the Vietnam era. After that, he resumed his formal education, earning an associate's degree in Computer Science from the Community College of Rhode Island. Later, while working full time, he took night classes to earn a bachelor's degree in Management from Bryant University. That preparation equipped him to pursue careers in Management Information Systems and Retail. He has held positions in computer operations, programming, systems development and project management. In the Retail world he worked both in sales and store management. Presently he is officially retired but is actively pursuing God's plans for himself and for the world.

Bob emphasizes that even though he applied himself successfully to the American tradition of working to get ahead, in between his two careers his life was remarkably changed. He describes that time as simultaneously both the worst time and the best time of his life. It was the worst time because all that he had been working for came crashing down around him. All the time, money, effort and heart invested in education, career development, family and home were all lost practically overnight. The American dream went bust, which left him in a state of despair and hopelessness.

Yet, in spite of all the negative things that happened at that time, Bob still says that it was also the best time of his life. While that seems virtually impossible, he is quick to identify the reason: that's the time that God intervened, making Himself very real to him. One day while lying on his bed awake and with his eyes wide open looking up at the ceiling, his mind raced as he tried to make sense of the many upsetting events going on in his life. Suddenly these thoughts sped up way beyond normal. What had been jumbled and confused instantly became extraordinarily clear and understandable. He describes how right then he had the sensation of his eyes opening again, though they were already open. At that moment he felt the presence of God standing right next to him. Bob recalls the shock, amazement and even the humor of the moment, as he said "You're real"!

From that moment on God was no longer a theoretical being who existed somewhere in the heavens. Not only was He real, God was with him in the midst of those difficult circumstances. That alone made it the best time of his life. Although Bob was profoundly touched and encouraged by that supernatural experience, he persisted in his own efforts to try to make right all that had gone wrong, but without success. Frustrated, angry and at a loss for any real solutions, he left home not expecting to ever return. Troubled by thoughts that what precipitated this downfall in his own life might also adversely affect others in his family, he considered that ending his life could be his best alternative. But again, God intervened as one day Bob felt like his spirit was being pulled on from the front of his body. He had been thinking that it was best for him to return home, so when that happened, he knew he should head back.

Bob pressed on, but six months transpired before that initial encounter with God became firmly rooted in a relationship with Him. Then within a few months, he became even more familiar with the realities of the spiritual dimension. The day after he received personal ministry at a church service, Bob experienced the ejection of a demonic spirit from his body. He recalls how his body was contorted and stressed, and how he had no control over what was happening throughout the process. The spirit was literally roaring in anger and in resistance as it felt like it was slowly but steadily being dragged out. With his own frame at a little over six feet, Bob could sense that this spirit being was quite larger than himself. Once it was gone, he could feel himself being filled up with the Spirit of God as family prayed and read from the Bible. Bob tells of a second demon spirit being cast out of him at another time, with apparent intervention by an angel, though in a far less dramatic fashion.

He shares these events now only to impress upon people the reality of this spiritual world, in the hope that they will begin to seek out the truth of it, and most importantly, do it in the proper way. He sees that most people don't even know that is possible, so he wants to help put these spiritual things in the proper perspective. Deeply disturbed by the reality that even many people practicing formal religions are unaware of these basic truths and are being misled by what they are taught, he feels compelled to make them available to as many people as possible.

In another incredible but beautiful experience, Bob describes how one day the Spirit of God came upon him and he physically felt in his heart an intensely warm and glowing sensation that was the perfect, unconditional and unfailing love of God. He believes that to be loved in that way must be the unspoken desire of every human being. No words could ever adequately describe it; something so rich in purity and goodness that no one would ever want it to end, and everyone should want to emulate it. Since that moment, his desire has been to become one through whom that love can flow. He is not alone in this experience as he knows of at least two other people who have testified to the same or very similar thing; and of the previous experiences mentioned, a great deal more than that.

But Bob stresses that the occurrence of such extraordinary events by no means overshadows the full picture of his journey of over 25 years. The God who came to his rescue years ago has never stopped being there for him every day. He says that the ongoing, life-changing, heart-changing process taking place, is no less remarkable and precious than any of the previously mentioned supernatural experiences. He knows God now as Someone who is close, not distant; Someone who cares deeply and is not in the least insensitive to the challenges in this world; Someone who is ready and willing to increasingly reveal Truth to the one who seeks it; Someone who wants to bring healing to past wounds; Someone who wants to be involved in one's daily life and provide the wise assistance needed to deal with it. This is the God Bob knows and the One he wants everyone to get to know. His desire is to help the hungry heart see the world with a fresh perspective that lines up with the reality of God's design.

∞ ∞ ∞ ∞ ∞

If you like this book and have found it to be helpful, would you please take a few minutes to post your review online? Reviews are very useful to getting any book noticed, and they just may lead others to learn about **Essential Spiritual Truth.** This information (God's words, not the author's) needs to get in the hands of many people as soon as possible. Your words can help make that happen. Thank you. Your time and thoughts are greatly appreciated.

Also, if your life was significantly impacted by the information presented here, you are welcomed to share your story. While time constraints do not allow for a response, the author would love to read your testimony, which can be sent to Discover.Gods.Plans@gmail.com.

∞ ∞ ∞ ∞ ∞

www.ingramcontent.com/pod-product-compliance
Lightning Source LLC
Chambersburg PA
CBHW060826050426
42453CB00008B/603